The Information Payoff

The Manager's Concise Guide to Making PC Communications Work

William Eager

D1547953

Foreword by
Alfred Glossbrenner

Prentice Hall PTR
Englewood Cliffs, New Jersey 07632

Library of Congress Cataloging-in-Publication Data

Eager, William, 1957–
  The Information Payoff : the manager's concise guide to making pc communications work / William Eager.
    p. cm.
  Includes bibliographical references and index.
  ISBN 0-13-158296-8
  1. Business Enterprises—Communication systems—Management.
  2. Information technology.   3. Local area networks (Computer networks) 4. Wide area networks
    (Computer networks)
  5. Management information systems.   I. Title.

HD30.3.E17   1995   94-3451
658.4'038—dc20   CIP

Editorial/Production Supervision: Lisa Iarkowski
Interior Design: Lisa Iarkowski
Acquisitions Editor: Mike Hays
Manufacturing Manager: Alexis R. Heydt
Cover Design: Design Solutions

The publisher offers discounts on this book when ordered in bulk quantities.
  For more information, contact:

Corporate Sales Department
PTR Prentice Hall
113 Sylvan Avenue
Englewood Cliffs, NJ 07632
Phone: 201-592-2863
FAX: 201-592-2249.

Printed in the United States of America

10 9 8 7 6 5 4 3 2 1

ISBN 0-13-158296-8

Prentice-Hall International (UK) Limited, London
Prentice-Hall of Australia Pty. Limited, Sydney
Prentice-Hall of Canada, Inc., Toronto
Prentice-Hall Hispanoamericana S.A., Mexico
Prentice-Hall of India Private Limited, New Delhi
Prentice-Hall of Japan, Inc., Tokyo
Simon & Schuster Asia Pte. Ltd., Singapore
Editora Prentice-Hall do Brasil, Ltda., Rio de Janeiro

Dedicated to
Samuel and Muriel Eager
Ethel Bell
Gerald, Patricia and Phil Eager
Laurie

Contents

2

The Management and Flow
of Information and Data
43

To prevent information overload, electronic communication must be managed and organized so employees can efficiently find what they are looking for. Communication software offers sorting and delivery options that help manage information delivered via databases, online services and CD-ROMs.

3

Remote No Longer, or I Want It Now
67

By eliminating barriers to communication based on geographic separation, telecommunication plays a vital role in creating the global marketplace of the 1990s. The incredible speed, quantity and 24-hour delivery of information dramatically change individual work habits and organizational performance. The Internet, synonymous with the information superhighway, is a global communication network that has recently opened its doors to commercial applications. Small, remote companies now go head-to-head with international giants. Case studies offer insight into what works and what does not.

4

Is the Door Closed?
Gatekeeping, Security, and Liability
91

Computer networks inherently create opportunities for unwanted access to information and data. Resulting security problems, as well as a flood of electronic information, can actually reduce productivity, decrease the effectiveness of communication and breach security. Additionally, there are copyright issues to consider when creating and distributing electronic communication. Solutions to these problems are highlighted.

5

Talk Back to Me:
Two-Way Communications

123

Using electronic communications, organizations can instantly tally customer purchases from outlets around the globe, which provides valuable data for sales and marketing, manufacturing, customer service and purchasing departments. Internally, companies can use electronic communications networks to survey employee attitudes, share data on electronic bulletin boards and allow multiple users in different departments to simultaneously work on projects.

6

Multimedia Is Here to Stay

139

Technologies that were recently worlds apart converge on the workstation to enhance communications. In addition to brains, the personal computer now has eyes, ears and a voice. Multimedia enhances training, customer service, sales and communications by combining pictures, sound, and text in an interactive format. Better compression technologies, wider bandwidth and multimedia PCs enable companies to distribute multimedia, including video, directly to desktop computers.

7

Making It Work:
Implementation and Training

171

Successful implementation of electronic communications starts with a comprehensive needs analysis. To realize productivity gains offered by the technology, organizations must train and support system administrators, educators and end users.

8

How They Did It: Case Studies
193

Case studies describe how global organizations, BASF Corporation, GTE, Northern Telecom and Union Carbide, have improved their global performance with personal computer-based communications. Implementation, development, hardware and software, system features, administration, training and economic benefits are highlighted.

Preface

Technological revolutions occur in stages, moving from science fiction stories into research and development labs and finally into the world of industry and everyday life. One indication that the final stage has arrived is when the terminology becomes part of our common culture. This is where computer-based electronic communications stand today. The information superhighway, multimedia, electronic mail, executive information systems and on-line databases now appear regularly in national media, become a point of discussion during business meetings, even crop up during social gatherings.

The Information Payoff provides a concise, practical overview of the latest hardware, software, applications and benefits of electronic communications—the storage, retrieval and transmission of information and data. Large Fortune 500 companies and small entrepreneurial firms can use this technology to significantly enhance productivity, reduce operating expenses and gain a competitive advantage in the marketplace. All organizations in a company, communications, human resources, finance, sales and marketing, production and engineering are affected.

Companies now use computer networks to distribute electronic information to employees at sites around the world. In addition to words, data, images, video and multimedia can be shared electronically. Electronic communication increases the speed at which information travels through an organization; creates a tremendous quantity of information that often requires immediate analysis and action; and empowers individuals to send information and data across operational boundaries. These characteristics flatten hierarchies and bureaucracies, and enable companies to compete more aggressively in the global marketplace.

The technology encompasses the networks, hardware and software that enable the creation, storage and retrieval of information. The business applications and benefits are diverse. Imaging and transmitting electronic documents such as checks, insurance claims, personnel files and patient records reduces paperwork and enhances customer service. Electronic mail, on-line databases, interactive surveys and two-way video rapidly provide managers and employees with valuable communications and information in their office, at their desktop computers. Multimedia improves employee training and broadens the scope and effectiveness of interdepartment communication. These applications improve and automate workflow internally between managers and employees, and externally between companies and their suppliers and customers.

Through interviews with senior-level managers in companies that include American Express, AT&T, Federal Express, Hewlett-Packard, IBM, MCI, MasterCard, Merrill Lynch, Microsoft and Sears, *The Information Payoff* provides readers specific examples of how large and small companies implement and use electronic communications to improve their position in the marketplace. The final chapter includes detailed case studies that describe how several international companies, BASF Corporation, GTE, Northern Telecom and Union Carbide improve productivity with electronic communications. These case studies highlight implementation, development, hardware and software, system features, security, technical administration, training and economic benefits.

After reading *The Information Payoff* you will be familiar with the technology, applications and benefits of electronic communication. You will understand why the information revolution just keeps on rolling, where it is headed and how computer-based communications can be used to enhance all functions and organizations in a company - including yours!

I would like to acknowledge the tremendous assistance that all of the companies highlighted in this book have provided, as well as the individuals whom I interviewed for their valuable time and dedication to the continuous development and improvement of electronic communications. I would also like to thank Carol Nelson for her assistance in fine-tuning the manuscript; my wife, Laurie, for helping with anything that needed to be done - love you; and my editor, Mike Hays, who has great ideas, maintains a strong belief in the merit and value of the information presented herein and is easy to reach (especially electronically). Enjoy.

Foreword

Around here, only the help pounds the keyboard.

That phrase has stuck in my mind from the day I encountered it over a decade ago in a *Wall Street Journal* article. The article was about how executives and managers were reacting to what was then a very new device—the personal computer.

What a perfect way, I thought, to begin a Foreword to Bill Eager's wonderful book about how today's managers can make personal computer communications really work. How far we all have come in those 10 years, and all that.

Naturally, though, I wanted to be able to cite the date of the article, and possibly quote even more of it. Who knows? There might be another quote or statistic that would even more sharply define the differences between then and now. So I signed on to Dow Jones News/Retrieval (DJN/R), the exclusive electronic home of the *Wall Street Journal*, and searched for that phrase.

Nothing.

I either came up empty or got hits on articles that clearly had nothing to do with executive cyberphobia. So I tried "typewriters" and "executives." That got me an article about

Smith Corona and Brother Industries, one about ergonomics in computerized offices and an obituary for IBM's Thomas Watson, Jr. All perfect matches to my search, but not at all what I had in mind.

I batted around some more, trying different search strategies and databases. And I did find numerous articles on executive cyberphobia. But I couldn't find the one article I was looking for. Maybe it wasn't in the *Wall Street Journal* after all? Had I perhaps misremembered the phrase? Oh, come on, it has to be here!

Finally, I gave up. I signed off the system and trudged up to the third floor to consult my conventional, low-tech files of paper printouts and clippings. They made for interesting reading. Among other things, they confirmed something I had noticed during my online search: Throughout the 1980s, "executives resisting personal computers and technology" was a stock piece in the general-interest press. After about 1990, however, those articles stopped.

I never did find the article I was looking for. I'm sure it's in my paper files someplace. I know I could hire a professional information broker to find it for me. In short, if it exists, I know it can be found. But I also know that the game is not worth the candle.

I also now know why I couldn't find the article I wanted on Dow Jones News/Retrieval, for it finally occurred to me to check how far back its coverage goes. Turns out coverage of the *Wall Street Journal* on DJN/R starts with January, 1984. What I was looking for would have been published several years earlier.

A *Perfect* Illustration

I've told you all this for a reason. Normally I would never reveal tradecraft of this sort, especially when it ends with my failure to locate the information I was going after. I much prefer to be seen as the online wizard who knows exactly which keys to press to winkle some tender morsel of information out of its database shell.

But the fact is that this episode offers a perfect illustration of why, regardless of your business, if you manage an enterprise, you need this book. It distills and presents with style and wit what it took me years to learn. I had to spend over a decade reading and writing about technology to reach the point where I knew that the information I wanted could probably be found online, which database was most likely to have it and, most important of all, when it was time to quit and try something else. But you can develop that kind of sophistication and awareness merely by reading this book and taking its lessons to heart.

My hard-won experience has also taught me to keep technology in perspective. After all, technology is just a tool. An extremely powerful tool, to be sure, but like all tools, it has its limits. In this case, the limit was the starting date of coverage in the database. Elsewhere, there might be a limit on the length of electronic mail messages. Or you might discover that your current equipment does not have the power to display full-motion video.

The key point is to be aware that such limits exist and to look for them before you conclude that the technology doesn't work, or that lack of success is somehow your fault. As I have said, it's taken me years to reach this point. But with *The Information Payoff,* you yourself will reach it in a couple hundred pages. You will quickly learn to use information technology as naturally as you would any other tool. You'll learn how and where to look for the limits and thus develop a pretty good idea of what the technology can and cannot do for business.

Equally important, you'll learn how to count the cost. And thanks to Bill Eager, you will have the understanding to say with assurance that this or that technology simply isn't worth the cost—or has such potential for the company that it should be implemented immediately.

The Pure, Cool Breeze of Common Sense

That's what I like about this book. It cuts right to the chase and in clear, conversational prose gives you exactly the information you need to have. It delivers more pure, blessed understanding per page than most books twice its size. This alone makes the book a standout. But even more important, in my opinion, is the clear, common-sense approach it takes to technology. Bill Eager knows that as a manager or executive, you don't have to know all the bits and bytes. Indeed, I often find that the minute technological detail so many other writers revel in gets in the way of real understanding. What you need—and what this book offers in abundance—is a knowledge of what's possible.

Thus, you don't have to know what commands to enter on Dow Jones or Nexis or Dialog. But in this day and age, you absolutely must be aware that these resources exist and that they have the power to search not only the *Wall Street Journal* but also *Business Week, Forbes,* hundreds of local newspapers, government documents of every description, patent and trademark registrations and nearly every professional or trade journal or newsletter you can imagine.

You will also find, to your delight, that this book strongly emphasizes the intelligent application of technology. In the computer and communications industries, there is a seemingly irresistible urge to do things simply because they can be done. Never mind whether it makes any sense or not. And, the industry being what it is, no one stands up and says, "Hey, wait a minute! This is ridiculous." Instead, the advertising and public relations machines kick in. Magazines run articles and columns about the product. Publishers may even bring out books about it. And those managers and executives who don't munch silicon chips with every meal assume, on the basis of all the noise, that there must be something to it.

They invest their time and money accordingly. But six months later, the product category is dead, and the industry is on to the next new thing.

This book will help you avoid that trap. Its clear explanations and seasoned advice will give you the self-confidence to evaluate technology. And that's crucial since, if you're new to the field, everything appears to have equal weight and equal value. And the heck of it is, there are really only two ways to get to the point where you know what really has value. One way is spend the years I've spent absorbing huge amounts of largely useless information in hopes of taking in a gem every now and then. The other is to stumble on a book like *The Information Payoff.*

As you finish the last chapter, you will discover that you can now analyze and evaluate the torrent of today's technology with a confidence and self-assurance you never thought possible. In a word, you will feel like you know what you're doing. And you will.

A Growing Sophistication

For example, you will not be in the least surprised that a knowledgeable person could search an online system and come up empty. You will know to look for the limits before blaming yourself—or your employees or associates. But, at the same time, you will also have a pretty good idea of when someone's trying to snow you.

Nor will you ever allow someone to suggest that paper files are a thing of the past. You will know that, as with the rest of your business, it's the result that counts, not whether you used the latest techno-wonder to achieve it. And the paper is far from out of date. Among other things, for example, magazine and newspaper clippings often have pictures and graphs. These are enhancements that the online versions of those same articles lack, and will continue to lack for years to come.

You will also expect to see a given information or communication technology produce unexpected (and unpredictable) results. If nothing else, searching an electronic or CD-ROM database gives you a new appreciation for how many different meanings a given English word can have.

And you will be in an excellent position to determine how the results and the technology—whether it's e-mail, the Internet or multi-media—can help or harm the company.

Eyes on the Prize

Finally, Bill Eager always keeps his (and his reader's) eye on the bottom line. Whether he is showing you how the technology is likely to impact your people—and the people-oriented steps you must take to ensure its success—or alerting you to the profound problem of "information overload," he never loses sight of costs and benefits.

I suppose the tip-off is in the book's title. But frankly, I've been disappointed so many times by misleading book titles that I tend to ignore them. That's why I literally cheered each time I encountered one of Bill Eager's many cost comparisons.

How *does* electronic mail compare with paper mail and faxes? What about the cost of storing a megabyte of information in various forms of media? Yes! This is exactly the kind of information managers and professionals need to make intelligent decisions about applying the technology. Here's what it is, here's what it does (and does not do), here's what it costs, and here's how that cost compares to your other alternatives.

Then, to top it all off, there are the case studies in the last chapter to show you how others did it. Even if you feel you already know the technology itself, learning how BASF Corporation, GTE, Northern Telecom, and Union Carbide have imaginatively implemented personal computer communications technology is worth the price of the book.

Conclusion: The Time is Now

Finally, while I'm a sucker for a memorable phrase, I really hate peremptory admonitions like "Change or die!" Though, like all of us, I must acknowledge its central truth. I think, however, that reality is not quite so harsh. Change is inexorable, and you really do have to adapt or die. But it happens more slowly than many of us assume.

It's hard to imagine any executive today feeling so embarrassed to be seen typing as to say, "Around here, only the help pounds the keyboard." You're much more likely to find managers with "notebook-envy," looking around at the passengers sitting nearby on a plane or train and taking stock of who has a faster, better, more powerful computer than they have.

But it has taken over a decade to get to that point. Much the same is true today with personal computer communications. When I first experienced it in 1979, using a 300 baud modem to access a now-defunct system called The Source, I was spell-bound. I felt certain that the process would be the subject of a *Time* magazine cover story any day. I did not know it then, but the time simply was not ripe.

But it is now. Suddenly, everyone's interested in the Internet, and multimedia, and e-mail and online information retrieval. The time for personal computer communications has finally arrived! And with it has come Bill Eager's *The Information Payoff*.

It's an essential book. A book that should be on every manager's and executive's shelf. I just wish *I* had written it!

—*Alfred Glossbrenner*

About the Author

Bill Eager lives in Conifer, Colorado. With more than 12 years of communications technology experience, Mr. Eager designs, implements, writes and speaks about electronic and computer communication systems. Mr. Eager has been an editor of several national trade magazines, including *ComSat Technology* and *Communications Technology*. Mr. Eager is President of the Colorado Chapter of the International Interactive Communications Society. While Manager for the Corporate Communications Department at BASF Corporation, Mr. Eager proposed and helped develop a computer-based system that distributes hypertext-based multimedia information to employees at sites across the country. In addition to computers, Bill enjoys photography, hiking and skiing. Bill can be reached at: AOL/BILLE2000, Compuserve/74010,1511, Internet/Eager@sosi.com.

Introduction:
Why Another Revolution?

There is nothing more difficult to take in hand, more perilous to conduct, or more uncertain in its success than to take the lead in the introduction of a new order of things.

—*Niccolo Machiavelli (1469–1527)*
Discourses

Connect personal computers with telecommunications networks and you have a technological marriage made in heaven. It is a union that dramatically enhances access to information and improves communication between individuals. Managers, employees and students share words, data, images, video and multimedia. In short, this technological alliance transforms both the process and impact of internal and external communications.

The technology also challenges traditional organizational structures. First, it increases the speed at which communication travels through an organization. Second, it offers a tre-

1

mendous quantity and variety of information that often requires analysis and action. Third, it empowers individuals to communicate across operational boundaries. These characteristics allow computer-based communications to flatten structured hierarchies.

Organizations can take advantage of these enhanced communication capabilities and the resulting changes in organizational structure to improve operational efficiencies and compete more aggressively in the global marketplace. Specifically, organizations can:

> Increase employee morale and productivity
> Enhance manufacturing and administrative quality programs
> Create new business opportunities
> Improve cross-division/department synergies
> Respond rapidly to marketplace changes and control crisis or emergency situations

Technology in and of itself does not guarantee success in these endeavors. To achieve a positive return on investment, organizations must address issues that arise from use of electronic communication, and plan implementation and training.

The Information Explosion Continues to Explode

Are we being strangled with information? Adding a new document to the file cabinet doesn't seem so bad until you consider that American businesses add 2.7 billion sheets of paper to file folders every day![1] In the workplace, many employees spend most of their day working with information.

---

1. The Association for Information and Image Management.

Between 1986 and 1993 the number of workers who use computers in their jobs increased 48%, and in some areas of business such as finance, insurance and real estate, as many as 71% of the workers use computers for their jobs!

Information is not the problem. It plays an important role in decision-making. Companies have numerous documents, policies, customer information, orders and news that employees need to access quickly. The challenge is to develop systems that efficiently store, sort, distribute and retrieve information. As the quantity of information continues to expand, the need for structured information management increases. Computer technology and networks offer solutions.

Technology—The Mighty PC

Computer manufacturers have significantly improved the speed and increased the memory of computer chips. Simultaneously, fierce competition in the computer industry has reduced the price of hardware and software. These events have created an environment in which organizations can afford powerful personal computers for individual employees. The result is a substantial increase in the installed base of machines in organizations. According to the latest U.S. Department of Commerce industry overview, shipments of personal computers (desktops and portables) to the U.S. market exceeded 11 million units in 1993. The installed base of personal computers in the U.S. has reached a significant 70 million units. Growth is likely to continue, and its impact is only partially represented by the fact that computers and computing now account for 10% of the U.S. gross national product, a figure that surpasses the automotive industry in economic impact. The Department of Commerce report also notes that the number of individuals in the U.S.

employed by information services organizations now exceeds one million.

Move Over Mainframe...LANs and WANs

Computing underwent a tremendous evolution in the past 20 years. During the 1970s, mainframe computers were used to store vast amounts of data and process it quickly. Computer users generally logged on to run applications. This was called time sharing, because the mainframe computer would literally move information quickly between users.

During the 1980s, the personal computer revolution brought workstations directly to users. There is one drawback to these independent machines: it is not easy for individual users to share information rapidly or communicate with other users. In the 1990s, network computing allows users to share and connect to software and files when they need it. Local area networks (LANs) use a computing architecture commonly referred to as client-server. This technology distributes processing between clients (desk-top personal computers that request information from the server) and servers (usually PCs with greater hard-disk space that store data and programs shared by many clients). The LAN places the power of computing in the hands of end users, with the added advantage of rapidly sharing information between users. Figure I-1 illustrates this evolution.

One reason computer networking is evolving at such a rapid pace is that the technology enhances existing hardware and applications. From a cost point of view this makes it easier to sell the technology to management. An article in *Information Week* elaborates:

...unlike many other technologies, networks build on prior investments in mainframes, mini computers, desktop PCs, workstations, and telecommunications. Networks connect and extend the reach of all those previously purchased technologies, letting more users share in their value. With a network, for instance, mainframes storing huge amounts of data can be accessed company-wide. Data can be manipulated at the desktop, processed at the server level, and whisked across the world...[2]

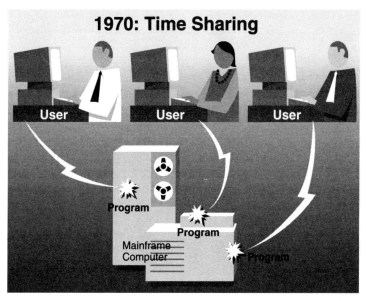

Figure I-1 (Part 1 of 2) The use of personal computers to access information and data has evolved from timesharing in the 1970s, to standalone PCs in the 1980s, to the connection of individual PCs via local and wide area networks of the 1990s. In a network environment it is easy to access, share and store files and messages between users.

---

2. *Information Week,* January 27, 1992 (no author cited.)

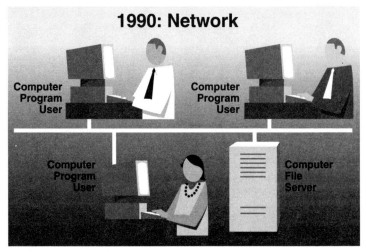

Figure I-1 (Part 2 of 2)   The use of personal computers to access information and data has evolved from timesharing in the 1970s, to standalone PCs in the 1980s, to the connection of individual PCs via local and wide area networks of the 1990s. In a network environment it is easy to access, share and store files and messages between users.

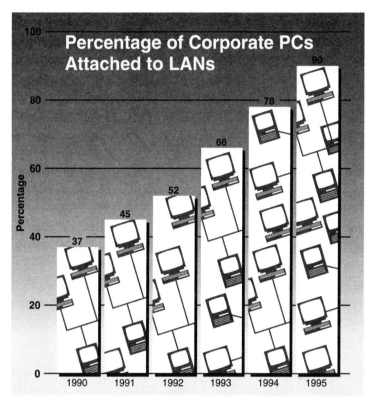

Figure I-2

LANS, like PCs, are rapidly spreading throughout corporate America. In 1990 approximately 37% of corporate PCs were attached to local area networks. Estimates suggest that number will increase to 90% by 1995. (Figure I-2).

The movement toward local area networks creates the perfect telecommunications infrastructure for internal communications. Productivity increases when employees can access a variety of software and information that cannot be stored on the desktop PC. The big advantage, however, is that interpersonal communications allows managers and employees to communicate via the personal computer, sharing messages, data and files. When employees at different sites need to communicate through computers, they must be connected through a wide area network (WAN). The wide area network is a logical extension of the local area network—LANs are tied to each other. Through the WAN, a sales manager in Florida sends client information to a sales representative in Oregon. An electronically imaged insurance claim moves rapidly through all phases and departments involved in processing; and when someone with a claim calls to check on the status, the customer service representative instantly pulls the claim, complete with digitized photographs, onto their computer. Likewise, senior management can simultaneously send a message to employees at sites across the country or around the world.

Software

Developments in software must be credited as much as those in hardware for creating new opportunities in internal communications. Recently developed software offers features that enhance communications. These include:

- ➤ Electronic mail with features that help compose and transmit messages and files.

- ➤ Multimedia applications that allow users to combine words, pictures and sounds.

- ➤ Hypertext functions that help people move easily through massive volumes of information, performing subject or word searches.

➤ Databases and spreadsheets that combine statistical information with flexible sorting and calculation functions.

➤ Knowledge-based or "expert" systems that help users find not only information, but solutions to problems.

➤ Groupware and workflow applications that let several people work simultaneously on electronic documents. It is also possible to automatically route documents and forms through departments.

➤ Dynamic Data Exchange (DDE)—A feature that allows different software applications to automatically communicate and share information with each other. For example, a word processing document can be linked directly to a graphics program with a brochure layout. Changes in the document are automatically updated in the brochure.

➤ Object Linking and Embedding (OLE)—The capability to link or embed data from one application into another. Linking creates a link to the source application containing the data, and embedding an object copies the data from the source application into the document. For example, a word processing document can have an icon that, when accessed, opens a spreadsheet program and displays a return-on-revenues bar chart file.

Applications

With global competition, organizations must improve operations to maintain profit margins. Product quality, research and development, customer service, purchasing and procurement, manufacturing, employee benefits, training, sales and marketing—every area of operation is challenged. There is one common element that impacts the success of new approaches to operation. That element is internal communications.

In *Thriving On Chaos*, Tom Peters provides some advice on what organizations must do to compete effectively in the changing marketplace of the 1990s. He writes, "We must look at what's working, and move fast to adapt and emulate the best. The speed of the transition is the most pressing issue." [3]

To remain competitive, organizational structures and operations must change quickly. Size is irrelevant. A company with thousands, or hundreds of thousands, of employees must be able to make decisions as rapidly as small firms. Companies realize that the organizational structures and methods of the past do not apply in the rapidly changing marketplace of the 1990s. Today's recipe for success: speed to market, rapid and wide-spread communication, quality, response to customer demands and close ties with suppliers.

Reengineering has become the latest manifesto to cope with the need for what is often a complete overhaul of business structure and operational procedures. Computer-based communication is indeed one of the main tools that will be used to rapidly and effectively change "business as usual."

Through the 1990s and into the 21st century, the evolution of information, technology and applications will continue. The evolution will have a direct impact on the ways that organizations communicate internally and on the ability of organizations to respond to competitive challenges. Managers face many issues as they evaluate applications, purchase technology, and sort information. The remaining chapters in this

---

3. Tom Peters, *Thriving On Chaos*, Alfred A. Knopf, 1987.

book explore the issues and technologies that managers must consider when they use advanced communication technologies to improve internal communications.

Electronic Communication Benefits the Bottom Line

Information, rather than oil or steel, is likely to become the most precious commercial resource, and the company that can gather, evaluate and synthesize information ahead of its rivals will have a competitive advantage.

—The New York Times

Managers and employees are familiar with two questions that inevitably arise when they try to launch a new program or process: "What are the benefits?" and "How much will it cost?"

Organizations realize a variety of benefits when they distribute information directly to desktop computers. Some benefits show up on the ledger book as a positive return on investment. Other benefits don't show up on the ledger book, but are as valuable as those that do! It is difficult, for example, to place a dollar figure on improved productivity, or strong corporate culture or new synergies created when different departments communicate. The issue, however, is not always whether an organization can afford the technology. If competitors, suppliers and customers develop electronic communications systems, the issue becomes when rather than why.

What Is Information?

Information is such a pervasive, powerful and valuable commodity that an entire industry has evolved around it. Founded in 1968, the Information Industry Association (IIA) represents approximately 600 organizations involved in generating, distributing and processing information products, services and technologies.

Association President Ken Allen believes that there is a strong connection between information and computers. He says, "We are rapidly reaching the stage where you can't tell the difference between communications and computing, much less between software and content. The Information Industry Association defines the content of information as the value and everything else about information as a commodity where an industry or marketplace enhances the content. The intrinsic value of information **is** the content."

An IIA annual report indicates where the content of information becomes truly valuable: "Information empowers. Information creates the power of choice—essential to decision making. And the quality of the information defines the quality of the decision."[1]

Organizations are happy to pay for information that improves the effectiveness of business decisions. Accuracy and timeliness are features that most often make information valuable. These features are critical in the financial industry.

Merrill Lynch & Co. is the holding company for the

---

1. *Annual Report of the Information Industry Association.*

world's largest securities brokerage firm, Merrill Lynch, Pierce, Fenner & Smith. The company provides investment, financing and insurance services. Total client assets in Merrill Lynch accounts exceed $350 billion. Front-line contact with customers occurs with 11,000 financial consultants based around the world.

Ritch Gaiti, First Vice President of Advanced Office Systems at Merrill Lynch, discusses the importance of information for his company. He says, "Our business is information and service. People look to us for information. So having information accessible for our financial consultants, having the right kind of information and having it be appropriate for each individual, is a strategic necessity."

By having instant access to information and communications, decisions can be made quickly at all levels of an organization. The payoff includes making correct decisions and saving time. Personal computer-based communications can save time that would otherwise be consumed searching for information. In his book *PowerShift*, author Alvin Toffler addresses the real, yet sometimes hidden, value of time:

> In addition to substituting for materials, transportation, and energy, knowledge also saves time. Time itself is one of the most important of economic resources, even though it shows up nowhere on a company's balance sheet. Time remains, in effect, a hidden input. Especially when change accelerates, the ability to shorten time—for instance, by communicating swiftly or by bringing new products to market fast—can be the difference between profit and loss. [2]

2. Alvin Toffler, *PowerShift*, Bantam Books, p. 89, 1990.

Technology Versus Information

There are important distinctions between information, information technology and information management. Technology alone does not guarantee access to or proper management of information; and information is useless until it is organized by an organization or individuals.

Organizations must first ensure that employees have access to information and understand how to effectively retrieve it. Educator and author Forest Horton Jr. explains the difference between understanding computers and knowing how to use them to get useful information. He writes: "Information literacy, then, as opposed to computer literacy, means raising the level of awareness of individuals and enterprises to the knowledge explosion, and how machine-aided handling systems can help identify, access, and obtain data, documents and literature needed for problem-solving and decision making."[3]

After organizations and employees access information, they must manage it. Helping clients manage information is one of the primary services of Ernst & Young. With operations in more than 100 countries, worldwide revenues exceed $5 billion annually. Services include the broad categories of accounting and auditing, and tax and management consulting. Ernst & Young uses information management techniques to improve efficiencies in financial management, human resources, operations and strategic planning.

A report by Ernst & Young details the successful implementation of information management by several Japanese firms. The authors note, "Information Management is some-

---

3. Forest, Woody Horton Jr., "Information Literacy vs. Computer Literacy," *American Society for Information Science Bulletin*, p. 18, April 1983.

times confused with Information Technology and/or Information Systems. While technology has transformed the various ways information can be acquired, stored, retrieved, and distributed, it still remains an enabling tool for the management of information itself. Technology itself neither produces, evaluates, understands nor adds meaning to information."[4] The Japanese firms interviewed by the authors have developed a set of processes, policies and procedures enable users to access information that is relevant to their specific needs in a timely fashion.

Information management transforms data into useful communication. Without structure and organization, information is useless and communication cannot take place. Consider an employee who needs to find out whether a certain medical procedure is covered by the company benefit program, or a manager who needs to know whether a press release about business mentions plant capacity. If the information they need is not organized and stored in a meaningful, easy-to-retrieve fashion, they become frustrated and unproductive.

For many organizations, information management and the resulting communication occurs in the communications department. Typically, communications departments are responsible for internal activities, ranging from writing, production and distribution of publications to marketing and library research functions. With PC-based communication, every department and every employee connected to the network has access to information. Economic benefits from improved communication occur across all areas of an organization.

---

4. Laurence Prusak, Ernst & Young, James Matarazzo, "Information Management and Japanese Success," Simmons College, November 1991.

Return On Investment

The Corporate Culture

One area in which the impact of electronic communication is difficult to measure but critically important is the corporate culture. The corporate culture defines how an organization performs business, internally and externally. It can be established by written or unwritten guidelines, and affects all areas of operation, giving specific guidance on the management of business and financial operations, research and development, environmental affairs, human resources and training. The corporate culture is important because it establishes an identity, a method of doing business that employees, customers, vendors and the general public recognize.

Any company or organization that has more than one office, location or site has unique communication challenges regarding its corporate culture. Large, geographically diverse operations make it difficult to convey to internal and external audiences both the written definition and the philosophical meaning of the corporate culture.

A demanding situation occurs when one company acquires another. Internal communications must convey the corporate culture of the parent company, often modifying the culture of the organization that has been purchased. Writer Richard Charlton addresses the role that communication plays with respect to the corporate culture. He writes:

> While defining a corporate culture might have ranked relatively low on communications needs lists in the past, the continuing wave of acquisitions, mergers and restructuring has made it an urgent necessity. Employees need and want to know what is expected of them in terms of the company's work ethic, and what the

company's position is on ethics, equal employment opportunity, and drugs or AIDS in the workplace. Employee communications plays a key role in fostering corporate culture.... By the year 2000, CEO's will be fully engaged in resolving the public issues that confront institutions. In many ways, management *is* communications. No idea, no strategy, no tactic, no policy, no procedure can be effectively implemented unless it is properly positioned through communications with those affected, whether inside or outside the company.[5]

The act of communicating information to employees is in itself a strong statement about corporate culture. The statement tells employees that management wants to maintain an open dialogue about issues affecting employees and the business. This improves employee morale and increases productivity. The briefings section of an issue of *The Public Relations Journal* describes the situation:

Companies including Federal Express, J.C. Penney and Hewlett-Packard have conducted employee surveys that indicate that well-informed employees are happier and considerably more productive than workers who are left out of the information loop.[6]

The sense of operational unity that accompanies a strong corporate culture also has a direct impact on customers. Clients receive comfort from the knowledge that everyone within an organization is moving in the same direction. Through electronic communications, managers and employees in different departments and at different locations can share information about the concerns and needs of clients. This type of

5. Richard Charlton, "The Decade of the Employee," *Public Relations Journal*, p. 36, January 1990.
6. *Public Relations Journal.*

electronic sharing promptly benefits ongoing customer service or quality programs.

Customer service is critical for success in the credit card business. MasterCard, Visa and American Express are assertively expanding their telecommunications infrastructures with the ultimate goal of improving service and sales. Master-Card International Incorporated (MasterCard), a New York-based payment systems company with more than $300 billion in annual volume in 1993, has enhanced communications and customer service by installing LANs in offices around the world. MasterCard uses both electronic mail and Lotus Notes as tools to improve customer service by facilitating internal communications for both project teams and problem-solving. As Director of Management Support at MasterCard, Karyn Mardis implements communications technology with business functions. Describing how electronic communication enhances customer relations, Mardis says, "We use it for employee announcements to keep everyone informed and for company bulletin boards which are used as repositories of shared information. We are implementing an application on Lotus Notes that stores data for members from various sources that can then be accessed from MasterCard offices."

As a global company, MasterCard's service extends far beyond North America. One of the wonderful aspects of electronic communications is that it provides a gateway for people with advanced technology, such as a computer connected to a local area network, to communicate with people (and countries) that have less sophisticated communication devices. Mardis explains, "Right now we have several mainframe applications that take information directly from a file, send it to e-mail, through our X.400 gateway to be delivered via e-mail, facsimile or telex (for members in more remote locations of the world). Communications within similar time zones is not usually an issue, but a bigger problem is solved when I can communicate easily between North America and Singapore. I prepare a document today and tomorrow I have a reply."

Keeping Everyone Informed

MCI is one organization that uses what it sells and practices what it preaches. The telecommunications giant employs approximately 36,000 employees at locations around the globe. MCI owns and operates one of the world's largest telecommunications networks, supporting a full range of domestic and international services. The company holds nearly a 20% share of the domestic long distance market and participates in every segment of the estimated $60 billion telecommunications industry. Its own internal communications are as important as the communications capabilities that it offers customers. Besides keeping employees informed, sending communications via personal computer helps MCI save money.

Sue Cushing, Director of Public Relations for the Multinational Accounts division of MCI, describes the use of electronic mail for internal communications: "A lot of important information is communicated over electronic mail, starting at the top with the president of our company. He sends out a weekly breakfast report that is a compilation of divisional updates of important issues and accomplishments. By reading this, executives and managers throughout MCI become aware of what's going on all over the country.

"Every morning we get a News Flash from headquarters. This report highlights news about MCI, our industry, our competitors, related markets and relevant regulatory or legislative issues. For example, if we had distributed a press release it would mention what publications picked it up. Or, if Congress was hearing testimony on industry deregulation, all managers would have that. Anything very important, including internal announcements or external events, updates on world crises, goes to all directors. Directors communicate with their managers, and those managers to their employees. We get the message across very quickly... Almost all of our employees are connected with electronic mail. Even if they don't have a computer in their office, they share a computer and access internal communication."

Crisis Communications

Rapid distribution of time-sensitive information or information that relates to changes in an organization is critical to success, in the eyes of both employees and customers. Consider this scenario: Your company purchases a firm that had previously been a competitor. A manager or sales representative is meeting with an important client, but has not yet heard the news. In the middle of the meeting the client asks how the acquisition will affect pricing or delivery of product. First, there is embarrassment; second, possibly the loss of a client. Significant organizational changes and crises demand fast communications.

Federal Express is a leader in overnight delivery of parcels and packages. Offering delivery services in the United States and 129 foreign countries, the company ships an average of 1.3 million express packages daily. Federal Express maintains a leadership position with an extensive internal communications network that combines video communications and electronic mail to keep approximately 91,000 employees informed.

FXTV, an internal video network, has been in place since late 1987. Daily, Federal Express broadcasts programs to 1,200 sites in the U.S. and Canada. Another 20 sites in the U.K. and

Europe receive monthly broadcasts. FXTV has several applications. The most noteworthy is FedEx Overnight, a daily six-to-seven-minute video recap of the company's daily operations. It is also used for company news. One report updates employees on operational performance. Information ranges from volume totals to service levels to the percentage of on-time deliveries. It details how sorting centers have done around the world, and discusses weather problems and service interruptions.

FXTV also provides traditional news items about new products, competitive information and operational changes. Another application is management communications. A monthly leadership program speaks to managers about issues such as how to conduct more effective performance evaluations, how to apply personnel policies, how to comply with federal aviation drug testing policies and how to manage stress and time.

Tom Martin is Manager of Public Relations. Formerly Director of Employee Communications, Tom Martin is extremely familiar with the FXTV network. Describing the impact of video and electronic communications on the bottom line he says, "FXTV used together with electronic mail really saved the day when bad weather in Memphis prevented planes from landing a few years ago." Effective crisis communications kept employees and customers apprised of the situation (see Figure 1-1). Martin recalls what happened: "That particular week in December, we had one of our worst weather interruptions ever. We had dense fog in Memphis. This happens about once a decade. It effectively shut down the airport from midnight to 4:30 a.m., our peak aircraft arrival and departure time. It caused two-thirds of our fleet to be unable to arrive on time… a terrible problem.

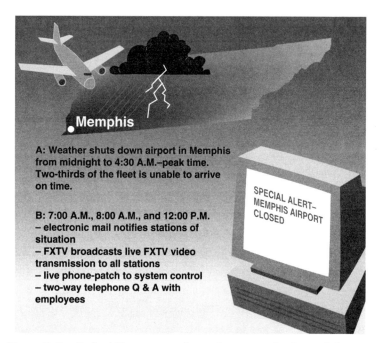

Memphis

A: Weather shuts down airport in Memphis
from midnight to 4:30 A.M.–peak time.
Two-thirds of the fleet is unable to arrive
on time.

B: 7:00 A.M., 8:00 A.M., and 12:00 P.M.
– electronic mail notifies stations of
situation
– FXTV broadcasts live FXTV video
transmission to all stations
– live phone-patch to system control
– two-way telephone Q & A with
employees

SPECIAL ALERT–
MEMPHIS AIRPORT
CLOSED

Figure 1–1 Federal Express uses electronic communication to help manage potential crisis situations.

"We went on the air live at 7:00 a.m. updating all of our stations about what was going on, what had happened and what it meant. We had a live phone patch to our system control center giving the exact flights that had made it out, how we were going to run the system. We talked to our customer service center, and told employees what they should tell customers. At 8:00 a.m. and again at noon we came back on with longer programs. We took about 30 minutes of questions and answers. The result was that by Wednesday morning we were back to close to normal operations.

"In that instance we used the electronic mail system to let people know there was going to be a broadcast. After the broadcast we did a written summary of the major content points. We put that out over e-mail so employees who couldn't watch the program, or didn't have access, could see the summary. Virtually 100% of our employees have access to a terminal. Every station hooks up with multiple computer terminals that can receive e-mail. We received many e-mail messages later that day saying 'thank you for keeping us in the know.' Many of our executives have said that these three programs alone justified our investment in the FXTV network. It is not something that on paper I can show you a definitive ROI, but if our executive management believes the network has returned the investment, that really helps."

New Synergies

Synergy, a buzzword that has crept into hundreds, possibly thousands, of annual reports, implies that the whole is better than the sum of the parts. By combining the knowledge, experience, production capabilities and customer bases of different business units, a company can operate more efficiently and accomplish new objectives that individual units could not accomplish.

Synergy does not occur by simply putting machines and people together. Synergy only occurs when an outstanding internal communications program connects people. The personal computer is a wonderful medium for developing synergies. PC-based communication connects employees at different sites or divisions and creates two-way communication. Employees share information and ideas with each other.

In many firms the organizational hierarchy of the past is breaking down. The pyramid approach to management has not proven to be effective in dealing with issues, such as quality improvement, that stretch across departments and operational units. As a result, some companies encourage the creation of networks or committees of people that functionally do not report to a formal manager. Electronic communication supports this flat organizational structure. This is shown in Figure 1-2.

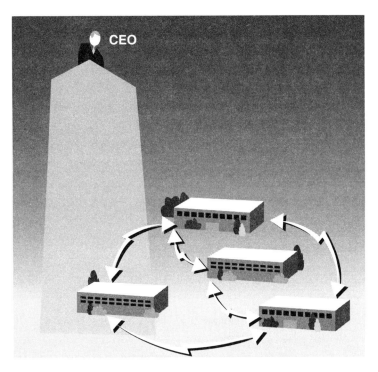

Figure 1-2 Electronic communications enable employees at all levels (and locations) in a company to rapidly communicate with each other. This flattens organizational structures.

Ogilvy and Mather Direct is the world's largest direct marketing agency. Its primary business is to help clients increase response for marketing purposes. Using a variety of media, including direct mail, television, radio and computer media, annual revenues for Ogilvy and Mather Direct exceed $340 million. As Senior Vice President, Martin Nisenholtz uses advanced technologies to help his customers improve communications. Noting how organizational structures can benefit from technology, he says, "It seems to me that as traditional hierarchies in corporations break down and many layers of middle management are eliminated, the formation of ad hoc and permanent networks to solve problems and fulfill objectives will increase dramatically. When you begin to implement some of these technologies, the productivity of these networks, in theory anyway, should go up dramatically. This is because the need to travel should be practically eliminated, and the result is the ability to obtain certain qualitative advantages over phone calls."

Paper Reduction—Let's Get Rid of the Paper!

Paper swamps organizations. The American Paper Institute estimates that annually, 22 million tons of paper, including printing and writing bond, are consumed in the United States! Industry spends as much as $100 billion per year dealing with this massive volume of paperwork where 45% of files are duplicates, 70% to 90% of files are never touched, and middle and senior managers spend as much as 45% of their time dealing with paperwork (see Figure 1-3).

Author Alvin Toffler notes that technology is one means by which organizations can both address the volume of paper and save money. He writes:

In one year the United States turns out 1.3 trillion documents—sufficient, according to some calculations, to 'wallpaper' the Grand Canyon 107 times. All but 5% of this is still stored on paper. Advanced information technologies, including document scanning, promise to

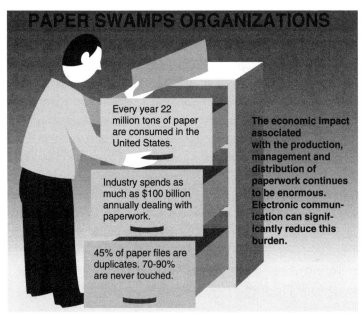

Figure 1–3

compress at least some of this. More important, the new telecommunications capacity, based on computers and advanced knowledge, makes it possible to disperse production out of high-cost urban centers, and to reduce energy and transport costs even further.[7]

The costs involved in managing paper are significant, and extend far beyond the paper itself. Other costs include:

➢ Hardware and printing costs involved with copy machines and desktop printers

➢ Maintenance of copy machines

➢ Personnel costs associated with the time it takes to

---

7. Alvin Toffler, *PowerShift*, Bantam Books, 1990.

> copy, distribute, sort, store and retrieve paper documents
> ➢ Mailing expenses
> ➢ Paper storage, which includes both filing cabinets, and the cost per square foot for office space required for paper storage

The tremendous costs associated with paper production and management have not gone unnoticed by Northern Telecom. With more than 57,000 employees globally and revenues in excess of $8.4 billion, Northern Telecom is the world's leading supplier of digital telecommunications switching equipment. Using electronic communications, the company provides employees and customers documentation for its product lines; it also routes internal communications and receives and replies to requests for proposals.

Tony Van Atta is Program Manager of Documentation Information Services. He believes that benefits can only be achieved after organizations determine where and how paper is used. He says, "The biggest problem in most organizations is that they have never actually looked at their documentation to see how things are organized. There are people to this day that are cutting and pasting the old fashioned way, making camera-ready masters. As a result, these documents actually don't exist anywhere in electronic format."

In fact, most organizations maintain a very small percentage of their documentation electronically. An article in Datamation elaborates:

> Companies are deluged by a wealth of in-house information, but only 2% to 10% exists in digital, machine-readable form. The remainder resides on desks, in file cabinets and in micrographic departments. The difficulties that organizations and individuals encounter in

their research efforts seldom relate to a lack of information, but rather to their inability to access it efficiently, if at all.[8]

Van Atta concludes that the 1990s represent a critical decade for companies to jump on the paper reduction bandwagon: "Coming to grips with this is something that will have to be done within the next decade if companies are going to continue to be viable and move to a cost avoidance situation. Ten percent of every organization's operating budget is paper, regardless of the form it takes. It can be a purchase order or a request for proposals (RFP). I just received an RFP from Honeywell. I'm not sending them back paper. I'm sending an electronic form. So you cut the paper trail off at the beginning.

"Everyone is realizing the advantages of electronic documentation. The pharmaceutical industry, for example. Do you know how much paper it takes to get a drug through the FDA? It's a tractor trailer full. The Department of Defense is another example. They will spend $6 billion on what is called the CALS initiative to reduce paper. It is a continuous acquisition and life cycle support system. Anyone who sells to the government has to deliver with the product, the documents it takes to maintain it, service it and operate it. They are absolutely drowning in paper. The CALS initiative covers a very broad scope to remove the paper from the chain. Not only paper that supports the product, but the paper that buys the product!"

The "paperless office" is a concept that dates back to the very first applications of computers. Although the dream has not yet been fully realized, recent developments in technology

---

8. Janet Mann, "Software to Manage the Paper Mountain," *Datamation*, p. 79, July 15, 1991.

make the concept more feasible than ever. One stumbling block has been the lack of high-speed networks that allow for rapid communication between different locations (and different companies). The ever-increasing global interconnection of computer networks makes it easy for companies to send and receive electronic paper, internally and externally. This trend will continue.

Software limitations have also plagued the 'seamless' transfer of data between users. The only universally standard file format is ASCII-coded text messages. However, when users want to start sending non-ASCII word processing, database, spreadsheet or graphic files to other people there is a problem. The individual receiving the file needs to have the same software package available on their LAN or PC. If they don't, they can't look at the file.

There are several solutions. One is that some software companies allow licensed users to send "reader" versions of the software to other people. This software allows the user to view, but not author, documents. Author John Warnock discusses another solution in an article in *Publish* magazine. He writes:

> The answer to this dilemma is 'electronic paper.' Two things are necessary to make electronic paper a reality. One is a device-independent format for a self-contained document, which can be transmitted to any computer at any location. The other is a reader or interpreter program that can display or print the document on any device. Like paper documents, electronic documents will be dispersed only in final form.... Electronic paper will benefit virtually all computer users, making paper-based publishing an option rather than an obligation. This new paperless form of communication can potentially change the main use of personal computers. Today personal computers are used pri-

marily to generate and prepare documents for printing. In tomorrow's world, the consumer of information will be the dominant computer user.[9]

Another expense associated with paper is the cost of floor space required to store documentation. When floor space is at a premium it makes sense to keep as many files as possible in an electronic format. Table 1-1 shows some typical costs for storing the equivalent of one five-drawer file cabinet of paper. The major factors related to cost are the location of storage as related to cost of floor space, and the storage medium used.

Table 1-1   File Storage Costs

Office		Records Retention Center	
As paper	$369.00	As paper	$30.00
As microfilm	3.00	As microfilm	0.26
As microfiche	0.40	As microfiche	0.04

Costs for storing 17,500 paper documents (equivalent of one five-drawer file cabinet). Annualized cost based on office space at $41.00 per square foot.

Table 1-2 shows pros and cons associated with three of the more popular forms of document storage—microfilm and microfiche, documents stored as electronic images, and documents stored electronically after processing with optical character recognition (OCR).

Microfilm and microfiche are well known. Electronic imaging scans documents and then stores them as graphic images. Users cannot manipulate or edit text from a document that has been stored as a graphic image. Through OCR a scanned document is processed into a file format that can be used to view and edit the text of the original document on the computer.

---

9. John Warnock, "Electronic Paper: Fulfilling the Promise," *Publish*, p. 120, August 1991.

**Table 1-2   Comparison of Features
of Three Popular Document Storage Techniques**

Feature	Microfilm/ Microfiche	Electronic Imaging	Electronic Imaging with OCR
Cost	Medium	High	Very High
Retention periods	Very long: 100 years	Long: 25 years	Long: 25 years
Retrieval frequency	Low retrieval	High retrieval	High retrieval
Works on network	No	Yes	Yes
Image loss	Based on handling	None	None
Image can be used as data	No	No	Yes with OCR
Image access time	Hours	Seconds/- minutes	seconds/- minutes

Saving on Postage

The ability to transfer files from one location to another is a excellent reason to connect computers on networks. Advantages include speed, maintaining integrity of information and cost. The speed of transmission is practically instantaneous. If information needs further editing or manipulation, users save a tremendous amount of time by sending it as a computer file. Information does not have to be rekeyed into the receiving computer. This process eliminates miscommunication caused by poor fax transmission or errors that occur when documents are rekeyed. Big savings on postage can also be realized with electronic communications.

Table 1-3 shows costs associated with sending a 100K file from New York to Los Angeles. A 100K ASCII file is equivalent to approximately 45,000 words, or between 120 and 150 pages of text—a long report or a short book. Using a 9,600 bits-per-second (bit/s) modem on a WATS line, it takes approximately 10 seconds and costs about 42 cents to send this file across the country from one computer to another. The latest technology for modems using standard telephone lines is appropriately referred to as "V.Fast" and operates at an incredible 28,800 bit/s. Long distance communication is fast and inexpensive. Now if employees could read 120 pages of text in 10 seconds, productivity would really increase!

Table 1-3   Cost to Send a 100K File from New York to Los Angeles

Means	Price	Carrier
Telex	$130.90	Telex 1
E-mail	14.75	MCI Mail
Overnight	9.00	Federal Express
Fax	7.20	AT&T
E-mail	5.00	Compuserve
Mail	2.90	U.S. Postal Service
Packet	2.75	Telenet
ASCII dialup	1.70	WATS (2400 bit/s)
ASCII dialup	.42	WATS (9600 bit/s)

Comparison of approximate costs for sending a document of approximately 120 pages between New York and Los Angeles.

Sue Cushing says MCI saves time and postage with electronic communications: "I can send a message to a colleague on the West Coast and get a response within hours or over the weekend or in the evening, so work doesn't end at 5:30 or 6:00 p.m., as in most corporations. People do have laptops at home. Or, if I'm home and the West Coast is still working, I can get a response before I go back to work the following day. That avoids sending first class mail, memoranda hard copy or overnight mail, which we did in the past. So you work faster and cut your costs."

The Cost of Doing Business

For the Japanese companies interviewed by Ernst & Young in its study entitled "Information Management and Japanese Success," the authors note that issues "such as how to determine the value of an information system or how to justify the investment and measure the payback of an information center become far less important in this environment. Information is a cost of doing business and justification and methodologies become pointless exercises."

Ogilvy and Mathers' Nisenholtz agrees, saying, "If you view the technology as fundamental, almost as a utility in the future, then it becomes strategic to test it and try to get it underway. But, if you view it as solving a very narrow problem I don't think it has any chance of success because it is too expensive. My advice to any company going into this today would be to look at it strategically. Looking at it from a very narrow point of view will not get you anywhere."

Electronic Mail—Rain or Sleet or Snow

Internal mail, memos—those wonderful manila envelopes that have the names of 50 coworkers scrawled on them before they reach your desk. Sometimes they move from office to mailroom to office, and sometimes they move from office to mail room to post office to mailroom to office. The interoffice note often takes more than a week to get from sender to receiver. Not only is this slow, but with the cost of internal handling time and postage (or overnight delivery), it is an extremely expensive form of internal communications.

This is why electronic mail, better know as e-mail, is growing as a method of internal communications. Users compose and receive electronic mail on their personal computer. It can be transmitted via a local area network or over telephone lines from one computer to another. Besides messages, letters and memos, electronic mail allows users to send computer files to each other. These files can contain text, audio, graphic and even video information.

Growth of electronic mail has been substantial. E-mail now has 28% market penetration. The Electronic Messaging Association provides users and vendors a forum in which to address technical issues and learn how to implement internal and external messaging. Association Executive Director Bill Moroney notes that the tremendous growth of electronic mail is directly related to the return on investment that organizations realize. "Organizations see electronic mail as a cost of doing business. That's why we've gone from 420,000 users in 1980 to more than 30 million today." Moroney estimates that by 1995, the worldwide base of electronic mail users will reach at least 50 million. Table 1-4 illustrates how several global organizations have a significant percentage of employees connected to networks and use electronic mail systems. Figure 1-4 shows the sharp rise in the number of electronic mailboxes in the United States and Figure 1-5 forecasts the economic growth of the electronic messaging market.

Table 1-4   Global Communications

Organization	Number of E-mail users	% Total Employees
American Express	30,000	46
Arthur Andersen Worldwide	35,000	53
Eli Lilly & Co.	20,000	67
Hewlett-Packard	82,000	90
MasterCard	1,500	82

As global organizations expand computer networks, increasing numbers of employees will use electronic mail for internal and external communications.

Electronic mail has many selling points. Two stand out: speed and cost. A message can be transmitted from New Jersey to California or Europe, practically anywhere in the world, in less than a minute. With this transmission speed, e-mail will certainly have as much impact on business communication as the ubiquitous fax machine now has. E-mail, however, it is more personal and effective because messages go directly to the desk of the intended receiver.

Rapid communication is important in all areas of operation, ranging from sales and marketing to manufacturing and customer service. Moroney elaborates: "Increasingly, business managers want an environment where products and services are brought to market more quickly. Simultaneously, organizations want to provide the maximum degree of service possible to customers. Communication, by definition, is at the heart of a lot of that. It provides a positive return on investment. Consider a legal filing, or a bid on a major contract. What is the value of getting additional information with the technology,

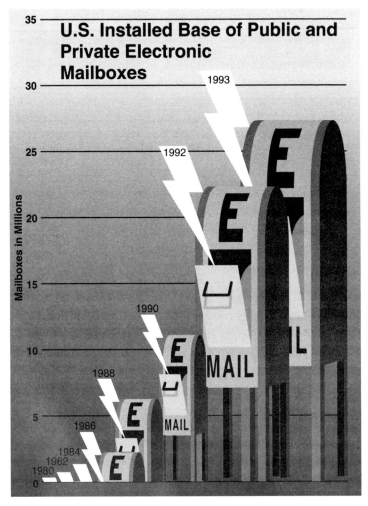

Figure 1–4   (Source: EMMS)

especially if the information is the crucial factor in making you successful? Obviously it's incalculable."

Information is important in all industries, including healthcare. With annual sales in excess of $5 billion, Eli Lily

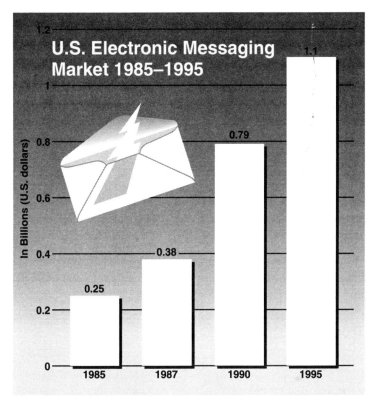

Figure 1–5   (Source: EMMS)

and Company produces antibiotics, insulin, antidepressants, and medical diagnostic devices, sold in more than 120 countries. Project Manager of X.400 Messaging Systems Dipak Shah confirms that electronic mail is an important communication tool for large, decentralized operations. He says, "There are several positive effects. First, people communicate more. Second, it helps flatten our organization. I can send a message to the CEO and I don't have to worry about going through a secretary. That is a tremendous advantage. It improves productivity because it eliminates telephone tag. If people are out of town, they retrieve their messages remotely. Business continues as normal even though they may not be in their office. And third, it helps people form common interest groups and communicate those interests effectively."

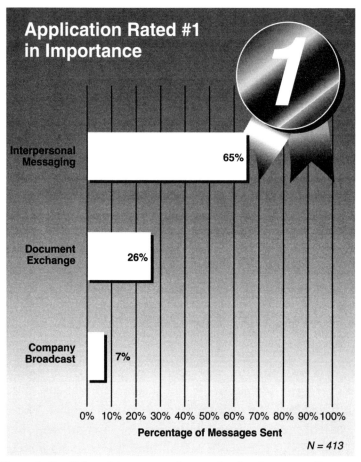

Figure 1–6　Although interpersonal messaging dominates e-mail usage today, other applications, such as document exchange, are becoming increasingly popular. (Courtesy Electronic Messaging Association)

As with most companies, the primary application for electronic mail at Eli Lily today is interpersonal messaging (see Figure 1-6). A recent survey by the Electronic Messaging Association indicates that document exchange is the second largest application of e-mail after interpersonal messaging. Shah implies that the role of electronic communications is beginning to expand. "We can use mail as a basic transport for any kind of communications, whether it be application to application, application to people or people to application."

Electronic mail is very much a LAN-based application. Beyond is a company that sells electronic mail software. Paula Berman, Director of Marketing, explains why companies benefit from putting electronic mail on local area networks. "Many companies, large companies in particular, have used traditional mainframe or mini-based systems. These systems had e-mail as part of them. In an attempt to what we call right-size, in fact downsize, people are moving onto local area networks. Local area networks represent an economical way to do business. E-mail is brought down to the local area network environment."

By connecting computers via local and wide area networks, large and small organizations enhance internal communications. This, in turn, has a positive impact on the bottom line, with tangible savings realized in mailing and paper storage costs. Electronic communications also has an economic impact in areas that don't show up on the balance sheet—areas such as corporate culture, employee morale and productivity. When the first question to be asked about using computer-based technology for internal communications is "Will it improve the bottom line?" the answer is a resounding "YES!"

The Management and Flow of Information and Data

Information's pretty thin stuff, unless mixed with experience.

—*Clarence Day (1874–1935)*
The Crow's Nest

Electronic information is invisible. Often, users are unaware that valuable information is available, waiting to be accessed. This creates a challenge. What techniques can be used to ensure that employees receive essential communications? This chapter examines how organizations envision the use of electronic communications, the ability of technology to solve information overload, and practical applications for the vast databases of information that are now available.

Push Versus Pull

Computer networks create an interactive environment where employees retrieve information. Historically, communications has been centralized. After being carefully tailored, communications were "PUSHED" out to readers. Now readers decide what they want and when they want it. They "PULL" in communications from a computer file server, a CD-ROM jukebox or an on-line network. This is a dramatic change for many organizations, but big payoffs can be realized by changing the status quo.

Organizations improve productivity in part by empowering employees to secure, access and make use of information. Bernard (Bud) Mathaisel, Director of The Ernst & Young Center for Business Innovation, uses an analogy to explain the importance of this new approach for distribution of communications: "One model of the CIO in organizations is as the chief librarian. One of the things that libraries did was flatten the social hierarchy with respect to access to information. Libraries increased access to information and learning. The parallel today is that the information technology infrastructure moves the concept of the public library into a new era for organizations. It removes the power of the few as it broadens access to information."

Larry Prusak, also of Ernst & Young, agrees, "What occurs is a bottom-up approach. People take responsibility for their own information. Executives get the information they need. They simply say, 'I need this,' and someone gets it. Everyone else is stuck with what they receive from finance, human relations, communications, a corporate library or information services. None of these choices are sufficient to provision a firm with the information they need for the 1990s. The technology opens information access to different layers in a company, which enables a firm to be remarkably flexible and powerful in using information. It is a tremendous infrastructure tool."

In 1991 GTE completed a merger with Contel Corporation, the largest merger in the history of the telecommunications industry. The company also announced that it would focus its resources exclusively on the telecommunications industry, exemplified by acquisition of 40% of the Venezuelan telephone company, Compania Anonima Nacional Telefonos de Venezuela (CANTV).

Major businesses include telephone operations; telecommunications products and services (including GTE Spacenet/ GTE Airfone and GTE Mobilnet); and GTE Laboratories. The company actively develops advanced communications networks to provide fiber-optic-delivered telephone and two-way television services.

With 117,000 employees, GTE takes advantage of the ability of personal computers to enhance communications. Brian White, Director of Employee Communications at GTE Telephone Operations, describes the new flow of information: "These systems enable employees to communicate laterally in ways that they haven't been able to in the past. The electronic systems that we have available enable us to provide access to information as opposed to dissemination of information. All of the research we have done seems to indicate that is what people want. Employees and the public at large are looking for access to information as opposed to dissemination of information."

The Information Pyramid

There are three categories of electronic communications. The first category includes information that employees access. This ranges from electronic newspapers to organizational procedures. A second category is information that needs to be routed from one employee to another. This includes communications such as electronic mail, forms, reports, customer orders and manufacturing bills of material. A third category is information that requires the recipient to interact with the communications, such as an electronic survey or a project management flowchart that needs signature approval.

The access category contains a wide variety of information, which can be conceptualized as a pyramid (see Figure 2-1). The base of the pyramid represents static information. Changes are made infrequently, information is not 'time-sensitive,' and employees don't access this information very often. Examples include organizational policies, procedures or standards. The base is stable and probably quite large. The next level of the pyramid includes information that is accessed more frequently (e.g. an employee benefits manual).

The next level represents a smaller amount of information. This information changes more frequently, perhaps posting employment opportunities, or a calendar of events. The next level might include the organizational newspaper, press releases and staff announcements, again updated and accessed more frequently. Finally, the top of the pyramid represents crisis communications.

All of the information, except that at the top of the pyramid, can be delivered most effectively when employees retrieve it. Crisis communication, however, requires immediate response. There are several ways to get the immediate attention of employees via the personal computer. The most effective is to send out a message alert. Either a visual pops onto the screen, or a sound comes out of the PC. Notification stays on until the user checks to see what the message is.

California-based Hewlett-Packard produced the world's first hand-held scientific calculator and the first desktop workstation. Today the company has more than 10,000 products,

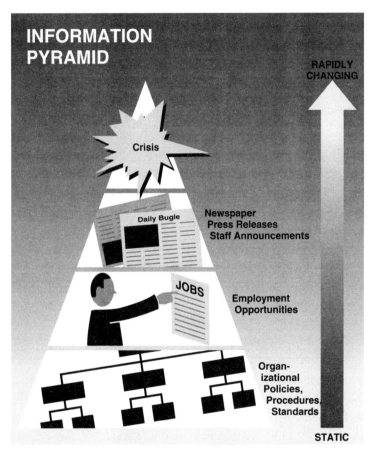

Figure 2–1

ranging from electronic measurement and testing equipment to mini-computers, printers and software. With approximately 90% of employees able to access networked PCs, Hewlett-Packard uses electronic communications as a major element of operational strategy.

Randall Whiting, Manager of Worldwide Electronic Sales Promotion at Hewlett-Packard, describes how certain types of communication are distributed to employees via the computer. "We have several electronic publications that we send out. Depending upon the audience, we maintain an on-line distribution for executive and senior-level managers. We generate periodic electronic news that gets sent out about once a week. For instance: This division has been reorganized, Joe Smith is the new general manager."

In other instances, employees determine the communication materials they require and access them. This is particularly powerful when an employee requires material for a presentation. They send in an electronic request for a certain topic, and the system automatically sends the appropriate text and graphics files. Whiting elaborates: "You may have a 2,000-name list and you don't want to send out information to all 2,000 people because they may not all need it. Consider a marketing manager or a sales representative in a remote office. They don't need to receive 10,000 messages across their desk. When they need information, they think, 'I wonder if there are any files that contains this?'

"We are switching from 'push' to 'pull'-oriented applications which allow users to find and access the information they need, when they need it. We utilize a number of pull systems, including some linked to our e-mail systems. This allows a user to send a message to a mailbox requesting information on a particular subject or to get some documentation. The system automatically sends the package of information which may include forms, slides or text. This is one of a number of online information services we employ to provide users the right information in the right form or media, when the users need it.

"When we send out our monthly publication, there is a list of the hotline material that is available. Users send an electronic mail message requesting a subject to the Corporate

Communications hotline. The system automatically transmits a package of information that has 10 or 15 slides (graphic images) plus the text of the script that goes along with the presentation. Instead of sending out a thousand of those, we only send out 100 or 150, and it is spread across time to those people who specifically need it. This lowers cost significantly and provides a greater service to users."

What's On My PC?

What will employees see on their computer screen to help them retrieve all of this wonderful information? To effectively help employees access the information they need, the user interface must meet two criteria:

> ➢ It must be easy to understand.

> ➢ It must rapidly direct users to the information or data they want.

Organizations must assume that employees have a wide range of PC proficiency. The requirements of different employees can be satisfied with a "user-friendly" menu structure.

Depending upon the type of network and computers, a menu can use text or icons. Menus should not have too many layers. Three layers are about as far as most people are willing to go into a menu before they get lost (see Figure 2-2). They also may get frustrated by how long it takes them to reach the information they seek.

Ritch Gaiti of Merrill Lynch emphasizes the importance of preventing confusion on the workstation. "We are trying to make it as simple as possible," he says. "The workstation and the phone are the two critical tools that our financial consultants have. Our mission is to drive as much as we can directly

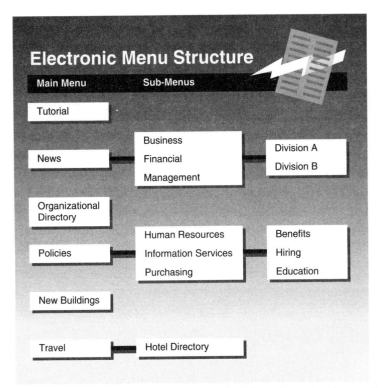

Figure 2–2   To make it easy for people to find the information they need quickly, electronic menus should not have more than three layers.

into the workstation; blend it so that different information from different sources appears homogeneous, and looks like it comes from one organization, when it may not; make it simple to use and retrieve so financial consultants don't have to wade through mounds of stuff. If there is overload, we have failed in what we have tried to do."

Beyond making it simple for people to find what they need, Gaiti feels that you can put too much information onto the network: "In a firm like ours, people are always competing for shelf space in somebody's mind. You are always trying to get their attention, and if everybody is trying to get their attention it is not going to work. There always has to be somebody who says no, or do less, or this is more important than that."

Electronic Newspapers

Electronic newspapers make a terrific first application for PC-based communications because most organizations already produce one or more employee publications. The process of gathering, formatting and distributing the newspaper is established. Also, most organizations already know how much it costs to print and distribute the publication. This makes it is easy to calculate cost savings that can be achieved by putting the publication onto the computer network. Electronic newspapers often succeed because employees are already familiar with the publication. They know what it contains and are inclined to give it a chance. In large companies, specific departments—sales, engineering, finance—may each produce their own electronic publication targeting members of their organization.

For the publication editor, there are other benefits. Electronic newspapers reduce the production time required for typesetting, proofreading, paste-up, printing and mailing. The deadline for story copy shrinks from two weeks before mailing to two hours before distribution. This added flexibility offers editors the opportunity to include late-breaking news.

Even after the breakup of Ma Bell in 1984, AT&T remains the largest U.S. telecommunications company, with annual sales exceeding $50 billion for the past decade. Each business day, AT&T's network control center in Bedminster, New Jersey, handles more than 115 million calls. Several things are falling into place that will keep AT&T in a leadership position well into the 21st century. With practically 100% penetration into homes and businesses in the United States, AT&T is strategically positioned to take advantage of compression technologies that enable distribution of images over twisted pair. An agreement with Novell will allow AT&T switchboards to communicate with local area networks (LANs). The $12.6 billion acquisition of McCaw Cellular Communications gives AT&T entry into wireless technology. Also, the number of miles of high-speed fiber optic cable run have increased from 5.6 million in 1991 to 16 million in 1994.[1]

In addition to revenues from long-distance telephone service, AT&T makes money from sales of computers and computer networks, enhanced by its merger with NCR. AT&T anticipates an increasingly global communications marketplace and plans to receive 50% of revenues from international markets in the 21st century. The company is also positioning itself with advanced computer-based communications such as AT&T EasyLink, which today provides electronic messaging and telex services for more than 160 countries.

Communications and computers are important to employees as well as customers. For more than two years AT&T has kept employees informed about company decision-making with an electronic newspaper. Marie Panzera, editor of *AT&T Today*, takes advantage of the immediacy of electronic communications. Produced daily, approximately 130,000 employees worldwide subscribe to the electronic publication. It is separated into sections for quick reading. There are sections devoted to company announcements, press releases, new products and services.

The electronic newspaper plays an important role in informing employees about extremely sensitive news. Panzera

---

1. Electronic Industries Association.

explains: "We have what we call *AT&T Today Flash Edition* that we send out immediately. We have used it during a service disruption to explain to employees what had occurred. Or, for example, during the NCR (now AT&T Global Information Solutions) merger with AT&T, we kept employees informed sometimes with a flash announcement because the news was so instantaneous.

"We distribute in the morning about 10:30 or 11:00. We pull stories from clips and wire services, and, because we have employees throughout the world, we try to pick up items from foreign newspapers as well. We provide excerpts from the articles, and employees can call and order full text."

What about employees who don't have PCs? Panzera says, "Let's face it, not everyone has a PC. We ask employees to display copies, and we have instituted poster boards where copies are displayed. There is always the capability to print out these things." Additionally, AT&T is now testing on-site kiosks, where employees who do not have PCs can access *AT&T Today.*

Sorting: Eliminating Electronic Junk Mail

With electronic newspapers, electronic mail and electronic databases, employees can access a huge amount of information. Confusion and overload can be eliminated if computer system administrators work with communicators and users to develop and maintain a well-organized menu.

Nevertheless, junk mail continues to move from the mailboxes of consumers to the electronic mailboxes of office workers. Electronic mail users now require sorting capabilities. As Managing Director of Public Relations at Federal Express, Tom Martin witnesses the proliferation of electronic mail in the workplace. "This is a hot topic," he says. "My own feeling is that it has real potential in improving overall time management. For example, if I wanted to send a memo out in the old way I had to go though multiple steps to get that done. I had to compose it, edit it, print it, copy it, physically distribute it. There are many steps along the way that tend to suppress sending out a lot of memos.

"Even with those barriers, many memos still get sent out every day. Electronic mail removes most of those barriers. It gets down to composing and pushing a button. Composing is almost an afterthought because it is so easy. You don't spend the time crafting an e-mail message that you do with a memo. We are just beginning to see the effects of this enhancement. I am spending at least an hour every day, sometimes two, working with e-mail, looking at letters, forwarding letters, answering letters. As a communicator, the good news is that all people are communicating more than when they had to rely on paper and pencil. The bad news is that messages, some of which may not be helpful, are proliferating."

The software industry has also recognized the need for information management. A brochure from Beyond, a Massachusetts-based electronic mail software firm, states:

> As electronic mail technology proliferates through an organization, users discover how fast and convenient it is. As a result, they then tend to overuse it. The more important your job is, the more distribution lists you are on, the more time you need to spend scanning through an in-box full of trivia. One CEO of a large corporation threatened to stop reading his mail when his in-box printed out 30 feet long! Uncontrolled electronic mail can waste more time than it saves.

Paula Berman, Director of Marketing for Beyond, explains that e-mail does not always represent a time/cost savings. Often, people could be more efficient if they used the telephone to make a call, rather than using electronic mail. BeyondMail software provides features that literally "go beyond" simple interpersonal messaging. The software helps employees process and route information, and helps organizations automate their information flow.

Berman agrees that message overload is one of the biggest problems facing users and organizations. She says, "Because electronic mail has so proliferated throughout organizations, and because technology has advanced to the point where these LAN-based e-mail systems can in fact communicate to outside public mail systems, we have information overload. People get lots and lots of e-mail, and lots of information is flying into their PCs, and there has been no way to prioritize or manage that information and filter out what's important."

Searching: Finding What You're Looking For

Searching plays another important role in managing communications received on the computer. Not only can the computer help users find what they are looking for; it can also provide direction for what they *should* be looking for.

Hewlett-Packard uses sophisticated search and retrieval applications to help users access relevant communications and information. Randall Whiting explains, "Many of our search systems use an interesting approach. Most retrieval systems are Boolean oriented—you ask for all documents with the word 'layoff' in them. Some of our search systems are set up to look for related topics and rank them according to the number of times the word or related topics is mentioned in the document. This is based on a concept of evidential reasoning. The more evidence, the greater the chance it is what you are looking for. For example, if a user wants anything that comes across on 'Printers' and it found the 'HP Laserjet,' then that would count as a printer. So you build your own knowledge-based synonym library based on what you want to look for."

Of course, it never hurts to give the computer system some guidance. Whiting explains: "You can also assign weighting to each of those attributes or logical connections. For example, I ask for 'printer' and Laserjet is priority 7, whereas an IBM Deskwriter is priority 2. The system goes through a document and adds up all of the hits. It then assumes that a document which has more information about the topics you are interested in is more important than one that only has a single reference to the topic. It adds up all of the weightings, and when it displays it on your screen it sorts them so that those which have the greatest accumulated evidence show up on the top."

David Fullerton believes that the speed of retrieval is important. He says, "All of the information technologies focus on the ability to search faster in a reduced field, get answers that you need, and eliminate data you will never use. That is akin to an expert system. It is the philosophy under which those systems are being developed, and it is going to get better and better."

Is there a downside to using computers to make communication decisions? Bernard Mathaisel at Ernst & Young believes that the current state of computer technology does not match the inquisitive thinking skills of human beings: "Computers can't replace (now or in the foreseeable future) the ability to recognize the emergence of new patterns. We can't say never, at least right now. What we have now is the ability to take tacit knowledge and create from it a reasonable expert systems filter. But it is current tacit knowledge defined by an expert on current matters. This will not replace the entrepreneurial mindset that senses new opportunities even before the patterns begin to emerge."

Databases: The World at Your Fingertips

Nowhere is the capability to sort and search information as important as in the world of databases. The growth of information providers is staggering, and indicates that the marketplace puts tremendous value on information. From 1980 to 1993, the number of on-line databases grew from approximately 400 to more than 5,000, and worldwide revenues from on-line services have grown to approximately $13 billion (see Figure 2-3).

The vast quantity of data and information available online plays a valuable role in internal communications. News from publications around the world can be accessed and incorporated directly into a format suitable for internal distribution. A writer for the *Financial Times of London* enters a story. It transmits to a news database. The publications editor in an organization gets computer notification that an article of interest is available. The editor accesses the article, imports it into wordprocessing or multimedia software, adds a few other stories and distributes it to employees at sites across the country. The process spans the world, and occurs electronically in a matter of hours...this represents taking advantage of the global village!

News is just one type of on-line information that can be accessed, analyzed and incorporated into internal communications. Daily stock market figures or summaries of financial news represent valuable communications for employees in treasury, benefits, marketing and sales. Table 2-1 shows the applications of on-line information for various departments in an organization. Three things must occur in order for an organization to

Figure 2–3 The number of online databases continues to grow, with worldwide revenues now at approximately $13 billion.

take advantage of on-line information. First, an organization must have a clear idea of the type of information it wants to receive. Second, a person in the organization must be responsible for retrieving the information and packaging it in a form that is useful for employees and executives. Third, communication must be distributed through a computer network.

Table 2-1 Application of Online Information for Various Organizational Departments

Data	Communications	Finance	Human Resources	Manufacturing	Research and Development
Text Information					
Articles	●	●	●	●	●
Bibliographic	●	●			●
News	●	●	●		●
Statistical information	●	●	●	●	●
Companies					
Aquisitions	●	●	●	●	●
Financial disclosures	●	●			
Geographic	●	●	●		
Number of employees	●	●	●		
Sales volume	●	●		●	

Table 2-1 Application of Online Information for Various Organizational Departments (Continued)

Data	Communications	Finance	Human Resources	Manufacturing	Research and Development
National					
Business patterns	•	•		•	•
CPI		•		•	
Employment		•			
Market potentials		•		•	•
Demographic data					
Age	•	•		•	
Income	•	•			
Population	•	•			
Directories					
Addresses	•			•	•
Contacts	•			•	•
Financial and marketing	•			•	

In an article in *On-line Review,* Barry Mahon elaborates on the benefits of distributing on-line information via local area networks:

> The most significant change in networking for the workplace has been the change from individual modems to shared (local loop) modems to workgroup PAD to the LAN. This development has paralleled almost exactly the growth in the use of PCs in the workplace, and has of course been driven by that and unfortunately not by commensurate growth in the on-line information market.[2]

Being in the information business for more than a century gave Dow Jones a head start on entering the electronic information business. Today, almost half of Dow Jones revenues come from electronic information and electronic publishing. Dow Jones Information Services, an operating group of Dow Jones, publishes *Dow Jones News/Retrieval. News/Retrieval* provides on-line business and financial news offering 67 database services containing articles and reference information. A partnership between *News/Retrieval* and Dun & Bradstreet made available the Dun's Market Identifiers database, containing more than seven million company profiles. DowVision delivers Dow Jones newswires, press release services and the complete text of *The Wall Street Journal* directly to desktop computers.

"There is an ever increasing amount of information available in all forms, electronic and print as well as others," says Richard J. Levine, Vice President and Editorial Director of Dow Jones Information Services. Levine feels that information is a valuable tool, but users need to put some thought into

---

2. Barry Mahon, *On-line Review,* Vol. 15, No.3/4, p. 141, 142, June/August 1991.

what they are looking for and what they want the information to do for them. He says, "Information is an important tool in today's increasingly competitive marketplace, and companies that use information well are going to do increasingly well. This requires planning, investment and an understanding of what you want to get out of the information system that you create."

DowVision is an information service that delivers a composite feed of seven news wires plus the full text of *The Wall Street Journal* to corporate computer networks, where software developed for that corporation searches these real-time information flows. Stories of interest to business managers or executives are delivered. "The system not only offers access to news, it also proactively delivers information," says Levine. "What happens if the market has just collapsed? Or a war has broken out? Or there is political instability in an area of the world where you are doing business? To cope with that situation, the *News/Retrieval* service functions like an electronic newspaper, and we broadcast headlines that alert you to major business, international and domestic developments that are not on any list that you have made. When you go into the service, the first thing you often see is a headline that is about the leading story of the day. Usage of *News/Retrieval* soars when there are major domestic and international news stories."

Dow Jones News/Retrieval gets its information from more than 1,400 sources. It is organized in 65 databases, which range from the full text of *The Wall Street Journal* to databases of company information from providers such as Dun & Bradstreet and Standard & Poors. Dow Jones also has a dedicated newsroom that prepares material for the electronic database. Figure 2-4 shows *News/Retrieval* reference cards.

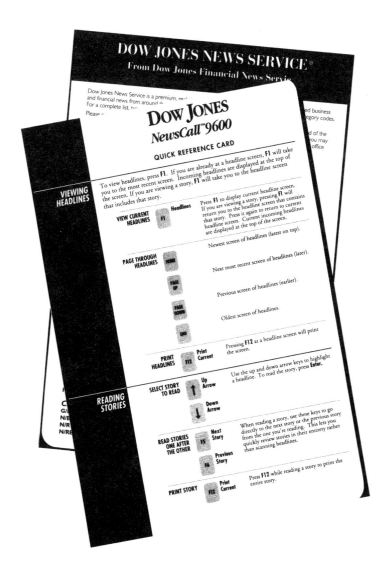

Figure 2–4 With more than 150 industry and news category codes, Dow Jones News Services provides continuously updated business and financial news directly to the PC. Simple keystrokes allow users of NewsCall 9600 to access headlines and hot stories, and perform keyword and time-of-day searches. You can even set the system to have your terminal automatically alert you when a story of interest is detected. (Courtesy Dow Jones)

Mr. Levine believes that the on-line availability of news and information can play a significant a role in the operations of small as well as large organizations. He says, "These electronic publishing systems have really democratized information flows, and they put at the hands of the manager in the small company the same information that previously tended to be in the hands of the large company."

There is no question that databases are a great equalizer in terms of business strategies and decision-making. Small firms now have access to the same news and financial data that were once the domain of large organizations.

CD-ROMs: A Lot of Information in a Small Space

Information technology continues to advance, offering new methods for storing and retrieving data. Computer-based CD-ROMs (Compact Disk-Read Only Memories) offer users a tremendous amount of searchable information in a user-friendly format. Just how much information? One CD-ROM stores about 680 megabytes of data, the equivalent of 1,800 floppy disks or 300,000 pages of paper.

Instead of using modems and connecting to databases, users access the CD-ROM disk. Software embedded in the CD-ROM determines the types of searches that are possible and the output capability of the information. A disk player can be attached directly to a workstation, or configured into a local area network for access by many people. CD-ROM jukeboxes let users quickly choose information from one of several different CD-ROMs. As with on-line databases, the number of CD-ROM titles continues to grow. The Optical Publishing Association estimates that as many as 5,000 titles were available by the end of 1993. In fact, there may soon be more databases available on CD-ROMs than on-line. The number of CD-ROM players in use is also increasing at an exponential rate. In early 1993, 466,000 had been sold. By 1996, the industry expects a base of 17 million. CD-ROMs also compare favorably to other types of media in terms of document production and distribution costs (see Table 2-2).

Table 2-2   Production and Distribution Costs of Information on CD-ROM, Floppy Disk and Paper

Media	Production Cost per Megabyte	Distribution Cost per Megabyte
CD-ROM	$0.44	$0.002
Floppy disk	$1.00	$0.39
Paper	$17.00	$5.80

Based in Golden, Colorado, CD ROM, Inc. produces and distributes CD-ROM titles, and manufactures and sells CD-ROM players. Company President Roger Hutchison believes CD-ROMs are the perfect media for information distribution. He says, "The decision-makers that we deal with have universally accepted the cost-effectiveness of communicating vast amounts of information to their people. I believe that more than 50% of the corporate 500 companies in the United States have CD-ROM projects either in the feasibility stage or ongoing."

"What is the purpose of an on-line system in a library or university environment?" he asks rhetorically. "The purpose of an on-line system like Dialog, which has four or five hundred different databases on-line, is to provide a form of archival service, or dynamic information to people that use an advanced communications system, some form of telephone, modem link-up. Today there is a decentralization of information, moving from on-line services which were recently only available through research divisions of libraries."

Addressing the issue of distributing CD-ROM information on a network, Hutchison says, "There are no technical obstacles to putting CD-ROM or other optical databases on LANs and WANs. By putting databases on CD-ROM and then connecting computers together, information is becoming accessible to individual businesses and government agencies within a building or an office. They have access to that massive database on the disk or on multiple platters." He adds, "We're currently on a project in which we are networking an entire country in the Pacific Rim."

The management and flow of electronic communication is quite different than that associated with paper-based communication. To successfully deliver information to employees through personal computers organizations must:

> ➤ Empower employees to put a priority on their communications needs.

> ➤ Establish an easy-to-use structure for information management. It must be easier to retrieve communications from the computer than from printed material.

> ➤ Take advantage of the unique communication capabilities offered by the technology, such as software that enhances searching, or databases and CD-ROMs, which provide a tremendous amount of on-line information.

Remote No Longer
or I Want It Now!

Telecommunications enables companies to move
information rather than people.

—*Eric K. Clemons and F. Warren McFarlan,*
Harvard Business Review

Convenience and service: two words that have transformed society. We can make financial transactions, purchase
gas, food and supplies instantly, 24 hours a day. With an
emphasis on rapid decision-making, competitive analysis, just-
in-time manufacturing and speed-to-market, the business
landscape of the 1990s creates an environment in which managers and employees expect instant fulfillment of their requests
for information and communications.

By eliminating barriers to communications based on geographic separation, telecommunication plays a vital role in creating the global village. Besides shrinking distances, telecommunication has also compressed time. Events occur faster

today partly because communication technology enables transactions to be completed within seconds.

Is Faster Better?

The first questions that organizations must address when considering the use and applications of PC-based communications are, "What are the advantages of rapid communications?" and "How fast is fast enough?"

Instantaneous communication is more critical for some industries than others. The financial industries depend upon rapid communications. Ron Martin, formerly Vice President of Employee Communications and Corporate Affairs at American Express, says, "One of the biggest challenges that companies have today is to communicate in a timely fashion. Any company that wants to be competitive in the global economy must communicate quickly to people throughout their organization. American Express is in financial services...markets change day by day, hour by hour, minute by minute. Being able to get information to people quickly is essential."

The rush to communicate is partly driven by the fact that national and local media receive and distribute stories faster than internal communications channels. A press release distributed via an electronic wire service can be transformed into a newspaper article or television segment faster than internal channels of communication can distribute the same information to employees at sites across the country.

In this respect Robert Bramlette, Assistant General Counsel for Sears, Roebuck and Company, echoes Martin's sentiments. He says, "One of the principles we adhere to is providing our people with information as soon as possible. Our goal is to get people to receive material and information from their manager in face-to-face meetings. We disseminate information from our headquarters to our units via e-mail or our video satellite technology so that managers are able to quickly receive and deliver the information to our people in a timely manner. The technology is a real plus."

The speed of electronic communications opens up new avenues of business decision-making. For example, in the past if an organization did not have an office in Washington D.C., they might receive information about legislative changes or votes after it was too late to make a difference. Companies can do things with electronic mail that didn't make sense before. For example, there may be valuable information about something that is happening in the economy, or a vote taking place in the legislature. With regular mail service, five days can elapse before the information is received. Electronically, the information is received the same day.

Keeping Executives Informed

Senior executives require fast delivery of information. For top management, information about business trends, manufacturing capacity, competitive strategies and employee issues can be quickly and concisely delivered over the personal computer.

In the United States 71% of executives have a computer in their office. This percentage compares favorably with Canada, where 64% of executives have computers, and Europe, where 59% of executives have them. It is also a dramatic increase from 1986, when only 45% of U.S. executives used office computers.[1]

Tremendous efforts have been made by software developers and endusers to create and take advantage of electronic data interchange (EDI). With EDI, electronic data is automat-

---

1. Steelcase Worldwide Office Environment Index from a survey conducted by Louis Harris & Associates.

ically transmitted, without human intervention, from one application to another. This can occur with one organization or between organizations. As an example, financial transactions between the purchasing department of one company and the accounts payable department of another can be conducted automatically. Or information about raw material, production and distribution elements can be electronically tied together. According to a research survey by Business Research Group, 53% of companies surveyed are using EDI, and another 17% plan to implement the technology (see Figure 3-1).

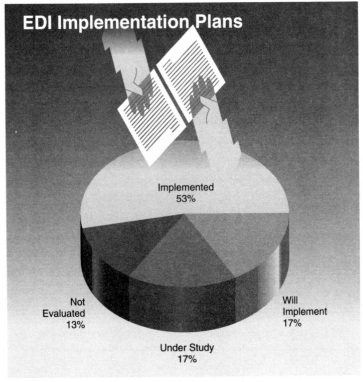

Figure 3–1   (Source: Business Research Group.)

This streamlines all areas of operation, and the resulting information can be delivered to executives at their desktop computers with an executive information service (EIS). Instead of waiting weeks for someone to analyze data and prepare a report with recommendations, senior managers can literally push a button to take a quick pulse of their organization. The EIS can be compared to the dashboard or control panel of an automobile. Using the computer, executives can quickly view a graphic representation of the status of specific organizational elements. They can, for example, view a bar chart that displays sales per division, or a graph that shows the relationship between access to raw materials and production output. If something is out of balance, executives can make decisions to correct the situation.

Payoffs from executive information systems are tremendous. *Information Week* provides one example: "Some companies are finding that the right desktop tools not only give executives a quick snapshot of where the company stands, but can help pinpoint where it's going. Pharmaceutical maker Abbott Laboratories in north Chicago, for instance, is rapidly progressing from the tactical use of EISs—for sales and price analyses—to strategic applications—manipulating numerical data to show the effects of future competitive decisions."[2]

Effective communication occurs when information is tailored to the audience. This is the approach taken by Merrill Lynch. "For our branch offices we have built our own system. It's more or less a one-way system, called FYI. It allows anybody in the firm to direct messages to any class of user," explains Ritch Gaiti. "So if any news or item comes up as hot, within moments we can get information to that financial con-

---

2. *Information Week,* February 3, 1992, p. 38 (no author cited).

sultant. We tailor the information to the individual receiving it. We try to avoid broadcast information because everybody receives everything; then you get overload. We let the sender of information send it to categories of receivers. That has been very effective. We also do that electronically where we scan our own customer files, and if we find any impending events in customers' accounts we notify the financial consultant about that. This keeps the financial consultant in front of what's happening, and every time they look at the information they know it's meaningful to them. We also have an alert facility so that as time-critical events happen, they pop up on the workstation and the financial consultant is alerted."

Douglas Brush, a partner of D/J Brush Associates, a communications research firm, agrees that an increasing amount of communications will occur via the desktop. He says, "There is a common trend toward centralizing on the desktop as much of the communications and information technology as you can."

Brush contends that communication systems do not themselves change companies. Instead, they help executives cope with changes that naturally occur. He says, "Corporate culture is being changed radically, not by the communication systems that are being installed today, but by the reorganization of American business. Restructuring, downsizing, elimination of many levels of middle management are making a bigger change on corporate culture than communications. When that occurs, communication becomes more important. Fewer barriers to communication exist, perhaps because the layers of management have been reduced. There is more dynamic on-line management in many aspects; every manager has either got a computer screen on his/her desk or one outside of the office. They get data and information from that at a very rapid rate. I would expect communications to take place at the same speed and in the same on-line dynamic environment."

Productivity Skyrockets When Electronic Communication Becomes Seamless

Initially, employees and organizations may find it difficult to exchange their pencils and paper for keyboards and screens. The transition to electronic communication is as much a cultural transformation as it is a technological improvement. The utility of computer-based communications increases as paradigm shifts occur in the way employees and organizations view and use these tools.

Electronic mail, for example, typically moves through three stages as it becomes integrated into the corporate work environment. In the first stage, managers and employees perceive the main benefit of electronic mail to be interpersonal messaging. As with its hardcopy counterpart, e-mail is initially a commodity where success is gauged by the volume of documents sent and received. Technically, in this first stage, employees may use different e-mail packages, connected through an X.400 gateway.

In the second stage, e-mail becomes an operational tool. Users recognize greater benefits than simply sending messages to each other. Electronic mail becomes a tool that reduces paperwork and improves operating efficiency. Departments and individuals establish working procedures that employ electronic mail.

In the third and final stage of implementation, e-mail becomes fully integrated into the corporate work environment. At this stage more than 60% of an organization's employees communicate with e-mail. Most employees use a company-standard software package. Advanced features of electronic mail, such as file transfer, distribution lists, transmission to fax machines and automated document sorting, are used on a daily basis and become the norm rather than the exception for communications. Figure 3-2 illustrates these three stages.

The transition from technical experiment to practical business tool can take two weeks or two years. To some degree, the speed of integration depends upon the size and geographic dispersion of an organization. However, firms can accelerate the transition by creating and enforcing company-wide standards for software and providing training and end-user support. Organizations only realize the full benefits of these technologies when they become seamlessly integrated into the daily activities of most employees.

Founded in 1913, the Arthur Andersen Worldwide Organization is the world's leading provider of professional services. The firm continues to increase its international presence, with representation growing from 54 countries in 1989 to more than 70 countries in 1994. The organization employs more than 66,000 people and enjoys annual revenues that exceed $6 billion. The practice of member firms is conducted in over 300 locations through two business units: Arthur Andersen for audit, tax, business advisory and specialty consulting; and Andersen Consulting for strategic services, systems integration, business process management, change management services, application software products and application development tools.

Andersen Consulting focuses on helping companies change to become more successful. One of the key strategies for change is the application and integration of client /server technology and computing. In keeping with the philosophy of

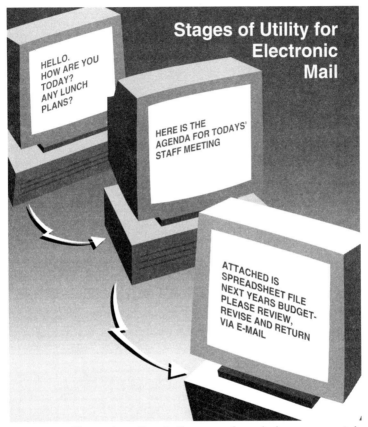

Figure 3–2   Electronic mail typically moves through three stages as it becomes integrated into the corporate work environment, first, simple messaging; second, transmission of information and routing electronic files; and third, full integration.

pursuing technology development, the Andersen Consulting Center for Strategic Research opened in California's Silicon Valley in 1994. One of the initiatives at the Center is the 'Infocosm'—the creation of a working model of the information superhighway. It is anticipated that technology capabilities developed through Infocosm will lead to new business opportunities.

The commitment to this technology is verified by the fact that more than 50% of the employees of Arthur Andersen Worldwide use personal computers. Eric Dean, a partner with Andersen in Chicago, oversees the implementation, operation and support of Andersen's internal information services projects. Dean describes how computer technology is becoming seamlessly integrated into daily business operation: "There is a big program that we embarked on a few years ago called Office Automation for the '90s (OA90) (shown in Figure 3-3). It is a program to put in place worldwide Novell Netware (a LAN environment) with Microsoft's Suite of Desktop Tools and Lotus Notes, all running on a frame-relay-based, multi-protocol internetwork. Lotus Notes has a combination of electronic mail and shared database capabilities. We currently have 22,000 users of Lotus Notes in about 20 countries, and hope to expand this to 40,000 by the end of this year in about 40 countries.

"Building on OA90, our line business units, Andersen Consulting and Arthur Andersen, are making extensive use of Notes worldwide. For example, Andersen Consulting has developed a large set of Notes databases and applications, collectively called the Knowledge Exchange, which are used to share the firm's experience which has developed around the world. There are systems that allow groups working in a specific industry or a specific technology in different countries around the world to keep each other abreast of the latest developments, wherever they may have happened. As a result, we can rapidly, efficiently and economically bring to bear what we have learned in one country to help clients in another country. We also have developed a Notes application that both of our

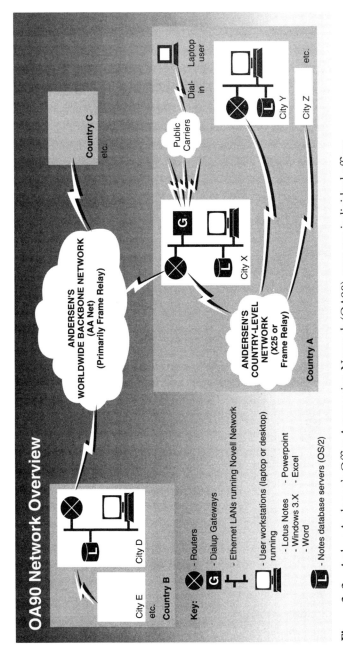

Figure 3–3 Arthur Andersen's Office Automation Network (OA90) connects individual offices (and LANs) around the world.

business units use to help track our massive training program worldwide. This system maintains an individual's training progress in local and self-study programs, and also handles scheduling and registration for all of our centrally administered classroom programs worldwide.

"Closer to home for me, we use Notes extensively in our internal systems group (ISS). One database we developed is called CINC—Consolidated ISS Notes Calendar. It is a database of all of the different internal systems projects we are working on. It contains details of all of the major tasks and individual work plans associated with the projects. This system helps coordinate the work of more than 500 people here in Chicago—everybody can log on and report their status. Employees, senior management and project managers who depend on the work of their colleagues can track the status of projects. This is a common repository for both executive information and for detailed tactical coordination and interaction among workgroups. We also use this database to coordinate the implementation of systems that are being deployed in all our offices around the world simultaneously. It is a terrific tool that enables us to coordinate dozens of group's activities with a minimum of noise in the coordination process."

Not only does this electronic communication system help Arthur Andersen pull together and coordinate worldwide activities, but, on a local level, it improves productivity in meetings and sets the stage for accomplishing tasks. "Everybody can read about projects before they go to a meeting," explains Dean. "This reduces the learning curve, clears confusion, eliminates excuses, and fosters and supports integrated activity. In other words, we have very productive meetings. Each Thursday afternoon all of the managers gather and discuss project developments. Managers know that during this

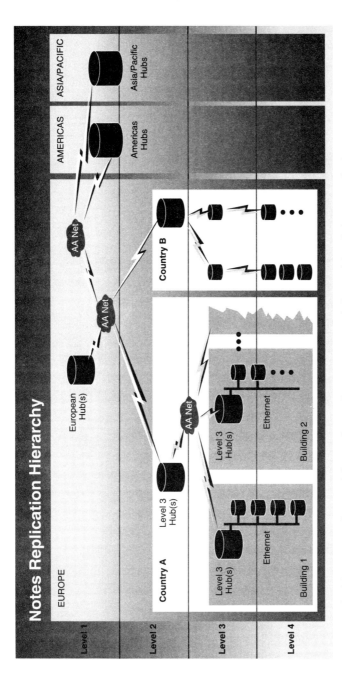

Figure 3–4 To increase the speed for sending information around the world and eliminate duplicate documents, the Arthur Andersen communications network uses a hierarchy with three levels.

meeting, if something is not in the database, they will have to explain it to the group. This ensures that the database remains current and that work related to projects gets done."

Technically, this worldwide network of databases is completely updated on a daily basis. For one project, Arthur Andersen may have people based in Manila and London as well as Chicago. They are all involved in implementation and need access to the same information, which is stored in a database. Dean clarifies: "In this example, there is a file server in Manila, one in Chicago and one in London that have a copy of this database. We have approximately 400 file servers in our Notes network. Well, I might make a change here in Chicago. There is a schedule when all of the databases in the world replicate with one another.

"The system has a hierarchy. Level 4 talks to level 3 every 12 hours and says, 'here's what I've got, what do you have.' They then exchange updates, replacing what is new. Level 3 then talks to level 2, then level 2 to level 1. The multiple level 1 servers then have three hours to synchronize with each other, and the cycle starts over again. If two servers both have an update to the same document, both versions of that document are maintained. In this type of 'collision detection,' all copies are saved. I can guarantee that any change I make here will be on every copy of this database in the network within 24 hours. This works very well for the types of application we are developing, but it wouldn't work for a customer balance record." Figure 3-4 illustrates this replication hierarchy.

Quick Response: It's a Must, Not an Option

With offices around the world, American Express copes with the cultural changes that must occur to make electronic communications valuable. Ron Martin says, "American

Express is geographically dispersed around the world. This provides a tremendous challenge to get information out to employees in 140 countries. Culturally, it takes effort to move people away from a traditional reliance on print and hard copy and the use of mail pouches and courier systems. American Express has a very well established courier and pouch system to all locations. But it can take from three to seven days to get something to some parts of the world. To the extent that the company is able to communicate more electronically and get people to use that as a preferred method, it enables the organization to share information in a timely way."

The technology forces communicators to respond quickly. Martin adds, "The technology puts a burden on communicators to make certain that we're keeping timely information on the menu. As a result, it becomes a habit for people to go regularly to a menu item like 'Hot News'…they will check it several times a day. Another technique is to do something that flashes or calls attention to important announcements. Some of it is cultural, whether people become accustomed to staying abreast of what's going on. As long as companies provide employees timely information, then I believe they will come to the source to see what is happening."

The speed of electronic communications often has a dramatic impact on both a company's corporate culture as well as its competitive position in the marketplace. This is true for Hewlett-Packard. The corporate culture is rooted in a policy that stresses open communication and idea sharing. Randall Whiting explains, "Without our electronic communications infrastructure, maintaining HP's unique cultural environment would be difficult, if not impossible. The technology also provides HP an enormous competitive advantage. Fast access to pertinent product and market information, combined with the ability to electronically communicate across organizational and geographic lines, maintains our ability to quickly react to market changes and new opportunities."

In fact, as an increasing number of companies accept and apply the technology, expectations rise with respect to faster and faster response and cycle times. Today, for example, it is practically expected that important materials, contracts and invoices will be sent overnight, whereas ten years ago it would have been perfectly acceptable to drop materials in the mail.

Who Needs an Office?

Organizations and employees also benefit from the portability and 24-hour-a-day delivery of communications. The ability to access information from remote locations provides communications to millions of telecommuters and sales representatives. Recent advances in wireless technology and personal digital assistants (PDAs), combined with an ever-increasing number of communication satellites, will allow managers and employees to literally send and receive messages, images and files anywhere in the world.

Gil Gordon, president of Gil Gordon Associates, provides telecommuting consultation to businesses and individuals. Gordon estimates that there are between five and six million telecommuters today. The number of telecommuters could grow to 10% of the work force by 1996.

Sue Cushing of MCI provides a clue to the potential number of telecommuters when she says, "There is a corporation, a Fortune 500 company, that we interviewed because we are interested in telecommuting. They said that in five years they expect 50% of their employees to be telecommuting. As a result, we are looking into services we can provide to those people who are going to work at home."

Technologically, there are several ways in which employees can communicate with their organization. Paula Berman with Beyond Inc. explains: "There are several ways that people who work at home can communicate with the company. They can do it if the company has a LAN, where they connect directly to the LAN. If the company doesn't have a LAN, they can subscribe to a service such as CompuServe, which has a large mail hub. You can use CompuServe's mail hub as the vehicle for interpersonal communications among members of your team. Very often people working at home are salespeople, they work in remote offices, and electronic mail is a great way of keeping these people more in touch on a daily basis."

Gil Gordon agrees that electronic mail plays a significant role in the use of electronic communications for employees who work at home. He says, "Electronic mail often plays a big role in telecommuting. If a company is already using it in the office, it becomes even more useful for telecommuters. Sometimes telecommuting is the impetus for expanded use of e-mail. You can get remote access to the LAN from home in a few ways. The only time I've seen technical glitches is in an application where somebody is working on the LAN or tied into the mainframe at the office, and they are accustomed to quick response time or file transfer. When they are working at home they have to go over the regular phone line. Even with a fast modem, they are going to operate at a slower speed than in the office. Whether that is a problem is often a matter of perception. If you are accustomed to getting a response in one second and at home it takes two seconds, that is twice as long."

"It offers a great deal of flexibility. It enables people to work at home, and it's going to enable companies to make better use of talents from the female work force," says Sarah Norton, Director of Marketing for the Massachusetts-based

Business Research Group. "One advantage of the portability that the technology offers is that more individuals are flexing their schedule and working some of their hours at home. Far-sighted companies that see and buy into that work environment have been very successful. From a standpoint of certain groups within the business community, such as salespeople and auditors, the ability to carry a portable terminal and put up diagnostics, statistics or data has greatly expanded the way they can do business."

Beyond the convenience of working at home, organizations can also save money by consolidating office space. These savings may not occur immediately. Says Gordon, "The returns tend to be long-term in nature. The office space cost savings benefit generally doesn't kick in until a company has been doing it for a while. If you have one person in a department of eight spending three days working at home, you don't produce your floor space savings. There are more companies that are beginning to look beyond the short term and beginning to understand what is going to be necessary to get through not only the next couple of weeks, but the next decade. The rules have changed for doing business. Telecommuting is one solution that can help businesses cope with the changes they are going through.

"Most of the growth in telecommuting is in small to medium-sized companies. They don't have the years of tradition and a six-inch-thick policy manual, so it doesn't take them as long to develop. As an example, I just got off the phone with someone at a Fortune 100 company that is developing a telecommuting policy. It has been in the works for at least four months. The policy is being circulated to more than 100 people for comment, and will then be presented to a human resource director's council. The bigger the company, the bigger the stakes. The impact on the bottom line with respect to office space costs and retention is a different order of magnitude for big companies, but telecommuting is not limited to them."

The ability to be in constant electronic communication with the office, from a car, a hotel room or even a client facility halfway around the world, creates a new paradigm in working that may dramatically change the way companies operate and hire new employees, and even impacts the manner in which they build new facilities. It is the concept of the virtual office. Taken to its ultimate form, a company that creates virtual offices would no longer need to have a dedicated office for Bob or Joan. Instead, there are office spaces that any employee could freely use when they need one; and, to further eliminate barriers between levels in a company, the office space for senior managers would be no different from the space available for lower-level employees.

Arthur Andersen's Eric Dean points out several practical advantages to the virtual office: "The idea is that we do not need our people to have a dedicated space in a physical building that is 'their space.' This is an everybody-wins program. People can work at home, on the road or from a client location. Part of the point is to eliminate the trip to the office. This frees up a little more access to your personal life. Of course, this process is easy to explain and difficult to accomplish."

Technically, there are still a few hurdles that need to be overcome before people can easily work from any location in the world. Says Dean: "I recently completed a trip to Asia and Europe. In every other country I needed a different cable to connect my PC into the telephone jack. In some countries, they won't let you have modem brand X. Today, there is a level of nuisance associated with the connection of the roving workstation back into the network. If wireless computing were truly ubiquitous, wireless access would be heaven on earth for the travelling user, at least compared to today's mess."

Ubiquitous wireless access becomes more real every day. An article in *Fortune* notes, "...dozens of companies are spending billions of dollars to build two-way wireless communications networks that will carry not phone calls but data—electronic mail, faxes, and computer files."[3] It is estimated that by the year 2000, wireless data revenues in the United States could reach $10 billion per year.

Telecommuting: Lose an Office and Increase Productivity

In addition to savings associated with office space, organizations benefit from the increased productivity that occurs when employees work out of the office. This has been true at Hewlett-Packard, as Randall Whiting points out: "We equip many of our sales reps with portable computers. The idea is that they can work outside the office. We did a significant study a few years ago about how sales reps work and what can be done to improve their productivity. One outcome was to equip them with portable computers and a number of software products. Not only can they share territory information, prospect status and communications with their managers, they also have access through the worldwide network to order processing so they can check on the status of orders, access product literature and create customer sales presentations at a customer's desk."

---

3. Kupfer, Andrew, "Look, Ma! No Wires!" *Fortune*, p. 147, December 13, 1993.

Gordon agrees: "You've extended the length of the work day. When you look at downsizing, typically companies have gotten rid of many people but have not eliminated a proportional amount of work. One advantage of having access to communications at home or elsewhere off-site is that employees can get away from the office. They can go home, have dinner with their families, do whatever they have to. Then, if they have to work at night, they can pick up their electronic mail or voice mail. They are no longer chained to the desk in the office. The advantages definitely outweigh the disadvantages, especially today when so many companies are operating on an international basis. The ability to pick up a message from somebody in Tokyo, who is just starting work when you're about ready to knock off for the day, means you avoid losing a whole day in the communication process."

Many organizations contend that the isolation created by letting employees work at home is counter productive. Gordon disagrees. "What we often forget in this notion of isolation and contact with coworkers is that what appears to be a benefit is often a drawback. One thing I hear from virtually every telecommuter is that one of their main motivations is they want to get away from the office, from all that interaction, because they can't get their work done. What starts as a simple question about work very often degenerates into a 15-minute bull session. I'm not saying that type of socializing is bad, but when you look at its cumulative impact on the work day, and put it against the backdrop of downsizing, you can see that people really have a struggle to stay even with the workload. Telecommuters tell us that in the first three hours of the day they will often do almost as much work as in a full day at the office."

A Telecommuter 'Speaks Out'— Electronically, of Course

Ken Camp is a Design Specialist who works for AT&T in southern California. Ken provides sales technical support to customers and salespeople for large-business voice systems. In several different positions at AT&T, Ken has been telecommuting on and off for almost four years. Ken replied to the following questions about his telecommuting experiences electronically.

① **How many messages do you get per day, and do you transmit files as well as messages?**

My e-mail varies from about 5 to 30 messages a day, plus anywhere from 2 to 20 faxes. I occasionally transmit spreadsheets, but more frequently they are imported into a word processing attachment, or a paper which is transmitted as a fax.

② **How does telecommuting impact your ability to stay 'in the loop' with other colleagues and your boss?**

I'm on my fifth boss in the telecommuting environment. They have all been receptive. And, with a little give and take on both sides, we've done well at adjusting.

③ **What are the benefits of telecommuting for you?**

I live in southern California. The first benefit is the elimination of a 140-mile-a-day commute. This holds my sanity together in indescribable ways, and aids the company in AQMD compliance with the Clean Air Act. I also am far more productive at my home office. A lot of the work is technical design. The quiet environment that I can control is more conducive to the sort of thinking that is needed.

The empowerment is more real than rhetorical. I control my work day entirely, and I control my productivity. In short, I have better control over my own success or failure at the job. Having all my records at my home office allows me to work longer hours when the need is there.

A Telecommuter 'Speaks Out'—
Electronically, of Course (Continued)

④ **Do you receive information while on the road electronically?**

I carry a laptop computer when I'm on the road. Until recently it was my personal laptop, but our organization is in the process of providing everyone with technology that there is a sound business need for—whether it be at a home office or on the road.

⑤ **What is the most difficult aspect to telecommuting?**

It varies depending on the work group and the environment. Sometimes it is convincing non-telecommuters that you are actually working. I get these "I'm sorry to disturb you at home" phone calls after I have already put in six hours of work. Convincing others that it is real work is sometimes a challenge.

Dialogue with other people can be difficult. It depends on who you're teaming with, and their level of comfort with the technology. It can be difficult to team remotely with a technophobe, but in our business, that is disappearing quickly.

⑥ **Other advice for individuals/companies that may be starting this process?**

Don't invest in obsolete technology. Be ready and willing to put funding behind the decision. People are more productive with proper tools. Ask questions and learn from the mistakes of others. Lastly, recognize telecommuters for their achievements, and don't forget these people who aren't with you in the office every day.

Technically, the speed of information delivery continues to increase as organizations and communication companies install new and faster telecommunications lines. As business becomes increasingly competitive and globalized, the speed of information and communications delivery will play a role in determining whether organizations succeed or fail. One competitive advantage created by the 24-hour-a-day delivery of information is the ability to allow employees to work out of their homes.

Is the Door Closed? Gatekeeping, Security and Liability

In the case of news, we should always wait for the sacrament of confirmation.

—Francois Marie Voltaire (1694-1778)

Corporate Communications— Dinosaur or Savior?

Every organization has a corporate communications department. Staffed by one person or several hundred, this department encompasses public relations, advertising, market research, employee communications and graphics/visual production. Structurally, the function of corporate communications is similar to two inverted funnels. Information from many sources comes into the department. The department then filters and distributes the information to internal and external audiences.

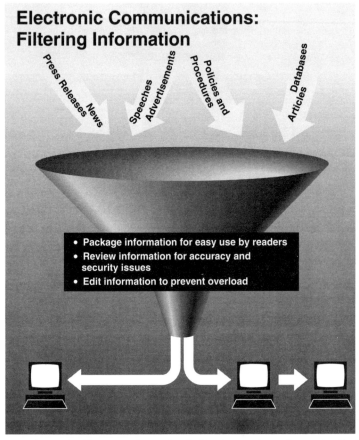

Figure 4–1 By filtering information before it goes into electronic distribution, companies prevent overload, eliminate security risks and make it easy for users to locate what they need.

Professional communicators perform three important roles during the filtration process. First, they package information into an attractive, easy-to-read format. Second, theyreview copy from speeches, advertisements and articles to prevent misinformation or proprietary information from being distributed. Third, they deter information overload by editing information prior to distribution (see Figure 4-1).

Until recently, it made economic sense to consolidate the talents of writers, producers, videographers, editors, typesetters and graphic artists into one centrally located department. Computer technology, however, makes it easy to bypass the communications department. A manager in human resources or research and development can write an article or a message, add graphics and transmit to all employees without consulting corporate communications.

This is classic good news, bad news. The up side is that the technology empowers employees to communicate with each other quickly, without delay or interference. On the down side, the technology potentially opens a flood of information that decreases productivity, dilutes the effectiveness of communication and breaches the security of internal information.

Some New Roles

The role of corporate communications as an information packager diminishes as the technology and ability to create powerful communication materials is distributed throughout an organization. It is impossible to monitor and control the production of communications throughout a decentralized organization. Therefore, a new role, that of communication consultant, becomes increasingly important. Professional communicators help managers in other departments develop strategies to effectively create and distribute electronic information. Once strategies are in place, the communications department steps out of the way.

Once a global leader in retailing, Chicago-based Sears has dropped to the number three spot after Wal-Mart and Kmart. Allstate, the company's insurance unit, remains the second largest U.S. property liability insurer. A 1992 loss of $2.6 billion initiated a restructuring of the company, including the sale of 20% of Allstate, the sale of Coldwell Banker Residential Group, and the 1993 spinoff of Dean Witter. The strategy for recovery has included closing more than 100 stores and significant layoffs.

With annual revenues exceeding $50 billion, Sears continues to be a major player in several industries, including telecommunications. In 1992 Sears entered into a joint venture with IBM to form Advantis, a voice and data network services company. Often, information that is relevant to one business unit is not specifically relevant to another. Nevertheless, Sears generates new business by cross-referencing its customers, and interbusiness communication increases sales and improves customer service.

Technology plays an important role in the distribution of communications throughout the various business units. Sears has widespread use of electronic mail, and more than 850 sites downlink video programs. Robert Bramlette of Sears notes, "We try to use technology in ways that permit us to better serve our customers. It helps us communicate quickly in both delivering and receiving information, and we are able to meet customer needs on a more timely basis."

As companies continue to expand local area networks and bridge existing computer systems, different departments within an organization begin to take advantage of the improved productivity that can be achieved with electronic communications. Often, this process occurs without input from corporate communications.

"Since every department in a company, particularly internally, needs to communicate with other departments and other executives, there is general usage," says Electronic

Messaging Association Executive Director Bill Moroney. "That is why you see adoption of electronic mail company-wide. The trend has been to tie together systems that sprang up internally in various divisions. What this represents is that corporations think it is extremely important that the accounting department be able to talk to the research and development department, which should be able to talk to sales and marketing."

The largest obstacle that organizations face in the development of an integrated network is the fact that installed software and hardware platforms are incompatible because they are based on the proprietary technologies of different vendors. In 1984 the CCITT, now the ITU Telecommunications Standardization Sector (TSS), a worldwide telecommunications standards organization, began to address the problem by developing recommendations for a set of international technical standards. Known as X.400, these standards describe requirements that vendors and organizations must use to successfully interconnect different electronic messaging systems.

The X.400 standard gives organizations and users the capability to send and receive many types of dissimilar data, such as messages, binary files, images, fax and telex. Today, most vendors have incorporated X.400 standards. Another set of standards, appropriately called X.500, defines a global directory standard that will eliminate the need for users to have more then one identification name across different e-mail systems.

According to Moroney, certain industries are leading the charge with respect to widespread use of electronic mail. He says, "The petroleum, aerospace, pharmaceutical and chemical industries and banking and retail products seem to be moving towards use of electronic communications. And now, government is increasingly becoming a bigger and bigger user. We are not yet in a seamlessly connected world, but we are very close. There are still a few minor hurdles to jump before this is as easy as dialing the telephone. Clearly, we are seeing the surge towards complete interoperability with the work now going on toward convergence of X.400 and Internet messaging standards."

Often organizations distribute communications functions (such as marketing) both vertically, through layers of management, and horizontally, between different divisions or operating groups. When this occurs, the most valuable role for corporate communications is that of information manager or facilitator. In this role, the department ensures that the flow of communication does not become a burden for users.

SRI International performs contract research and consulting for clients worldwide. Much of the work performed by SRI focuses on understanding the impact of technology on business and society. Computer technology is no exception. In a list of major achievements, SRI is recognized for work developing optical disk recording (1963) and the computer "mouse" (1964).

Cathy Flowers, Manager of Corporate Public Relations, believes that corporate communications should perform several roles. She says, "The department should play two roles, editor and facilitator. Organizations are not going to stay hierarchical. They have to be flattened, flexible and change-oriented. Anyone working in a high-technology organization sees that. Places without hierarchies move the fastest. The role of corporate communications is to ensure that cross-boundary communications are facilitated."

Internet: An Information Superhighway that Reaches Around the World

Editorial control, or at least common sense, is especially important in large networks that serve many users. The Internet is such a network (see Figure 4-2). Originally developed by the government, the Internet is an affiliation of tens of thousands of private, academic and government-supported networks. Global in scope, the Internet connects millions of computers, and as many as 15 million people in the United States and 20 to 30 million individuals in more than 60 countries. The Internet connects libraries, colleges, research labs, businesses and homes, often using telephone lines.

Only three years ago, the Internet was virtually the private domain of scientists, academics and students who used the network to share ideas and work on research projects. Today, however, the Internet is also used by companies for communications, marketing and business development. With international connections, electronic mail is a popular Internet application. Businesses users in the United States or Europe can get to a computer in Tokyo, Japan, in seconds without worrying about area codes, foreign exchanges or the time of day.

By joining the Internet, organizations save money on establishing their own wide area networks. Internet offers a variety of services and applications ranging from on-line databases to electronic mail. Vice President Al Gore has popularized the Internet with the concept of the 'electronic superhighway,' and President Clinton became the first head of state to use the Internet for electronic messaging on March 2, 1993 (Figure 4–3).

The Internet is undergoing significant changes in scope, operation and funding. The U.S. National Science Foundation (NSF) built the backbone for the Internet in the mid-1980s.

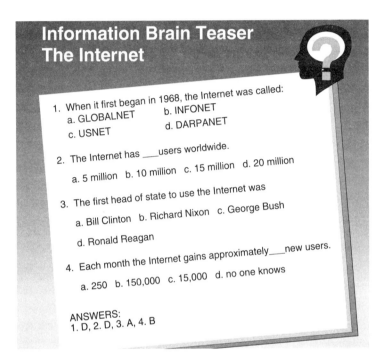

Figure 4–2

Today, NSF spends $24 million annually to operate the telecommunications backbone for U. S. research and academic communities. In so doing, NSF indirectly subsidizes other traffic on the system.

In 1991 NSF lifted restrictions against commercial use of the Internet. Combined with increasing awareness of the system, this opened a floodgate of new users. Now, every month the Internet logs on 150,000 new users. The convenience of using the Internet for international messaging and commercial activity has not gone unnoticed by telecommunication service providers. In 1992 Sprint became the first carrier to extend the TCP/IP service to its commercial customers under the name

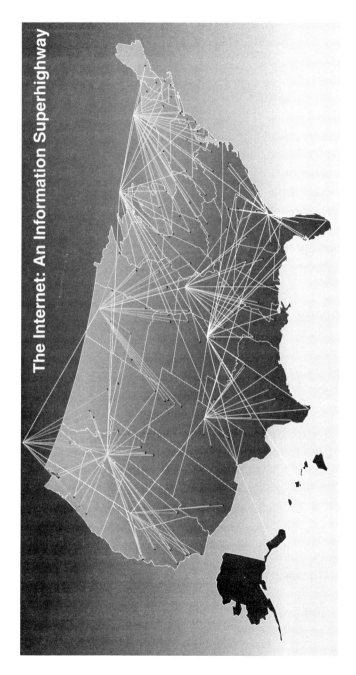

The Internet: An Information Superhighway

Figure 4–3

SprintLink. Others quickly followed. An independent business unit of AT&T, AT&T EasyLink Services, is a value-added network that offers a wide variety of electronic communications services, including EDI, bulletin boards, fax and telex transmission and electronic mail (AT&T Mail and Messsaging Services). MCI's Global Messaging Service and Advantis (a joint venture between IBM and Sears) offer similar services. These and other companies now provide gateways for users to connect to and transmit messages and data over the Internet. Pricing structures vary, with some service company fees contingent upon a certain number of messages per month, while others charge on a per-message basis.

Not to be left out, cable television companies are quickly positioning themselves to cash in on the demand for interactive information. It is an obvious avenue for expansion as the pipeline potentially connecting more than 90% of U.S. homes (and businesses) already exists. Relying primarily on revenues from the delivery of entertainment, cable operators have not focused on business services. This is changing.

Boston-based Continental Cablevision, the third largest multiple system operator (MSO), has joined forces with Performance Systems International of Herndon, Virginia, the nation's largest Internet service provider. Together they offer a high-speed link to the Internet over the same coaxial cables that carry television channels. Eventually, Continental hopes to offer this service to three million customers nationwide.

The price, initially more than $100 per month, may intimidate some users. However, the cable pipeline offers extremely fast transmission rates. Standard telephone lines (twisted pair wires) provide an average rate of 9,600 bits per second. Coaxial cable can carry 500,000 bits of information per second.

The increasing number of users creates ever-increasing traffic on the network. In September 1991, 10 billion packets of information travelled over the network. Less than two years later, in February 1993, 26 billion packets of information moved across the network. As an example of industry use of Internet for e-mail, during 1993 the number of mail messages carried by IBM and Digital's Internet gateways exceeded one million. This level of activity necessitates an increasing number of access points, greater bandwidth and an easier-to-use interface to the network.

Today, the major commercial and NSF backbones are T3 lines, providing 45-megabytes-per-second speed. In the next few years they will be upgraded to gigabyte speeds. The bandwidth on the Internet is large enough that compressed video is being distributed on the Internet today. In fact, with 45 Mbps there is only a 2-1 compression ratio. However, because this gobbles a tremendous amount of bandwidth, video signals are compressed further.

Technical upgrades and administrative activities may soon move to the private sector. Recently, the NSF awarded funding to telecommunications firms, including regional Bell operating companies and interexchange carriers, to operate parts of NSFNET. As this trend continues, the government may soon get out of the connectivity business.

In Colorado, individuals and companies access the Internet through the Colorado SuperNet, a broker for access to the Internet for the state. The SuperNet currently has 6,000 Internet connections for individuals and organizations. The actual number of users is much higher, though, because many connections are for numerous users. One company has 20,000 employees who get access through the Internet connection. Users range from entire communities to corporations, universities, libraries, medical institutions, even an on-line bookstore where users can search catalogs and order on-line.

Guy K. Cook is Chief Executive Officer for the Colorado SuperNet, Inc. Mr. Cook enthusiastically describes both the growth and business potential for the Internet. He says, "The Internet grows exponentially. It has doubled in size each ten months for the past six years. Today there are approximately 1-1/2 million hosts on the Internet. These are nodes—they can be mainframes, mini-computers or micros. Behind each of these computers there are thousands, tens of thousands, potentially hundreds of thousands of people who can receive e-mail through the node. One of the magic things about it is that you can connect with any type of computer. The TCP/IP (transmission control protocol/Internet protocol) solves the Tower of Babel problem because it is hardware and software independent."

A second magical aspect of the "Net" is that it is a shared-resource network. Translated, this means that each user purchases their own connection (or on-ramp) to this international network. Then, for the cost of a local call, an individual can transmit and receive international correspondence.

"It is safe to bet that in the next ten years virtually all businesses, right down to every employee, will have Internet e-mail addresses," says Cook. "At that point the Internet will be a business tool—one which is much more robust than the fax machine because it is interactive, offering users information search and retrieval functions. The Internet will have a far greater impact on society than the fax ever will. Corporate deployment directly relates to a company's corporate culture and how progressive the management is. The president of EDS, for example, uses the Internet all of the time, and probably fields between 5,000—7,000 messages a month."

The Internet represents an extremely cost-effective medium with which individuals and companies can reach out to the world. Table 4-1 shows the variety of line connections and associated costs for accessing the Internet. Cook predicts that business use of the Internet will continue to expand as companies realize the practical time- and money-saving applications. "From the order processing, manufacturing, sales and customer support standpoints, all business operations can use the Internet," he notes. "Once managers in these departments have this tool in place, they realize they can't do without it. Furthermore, they gain a competitive advantage by incorporating it into the organization. A great deal of traffic on the Internet now is purchase orders, invoices, orders, it's the most expeditious way to do this for people who 'need it now.' It is truly an advanced communications tool, a strategic weapon for companies."

Table 4-1 Various Costs and Line Connections to Access the Internet

Company Size	Internet Access	Approximate Cost
Individual or one-person company	Dial-up access	$15–$20 per month
Small company, five or six individuals	Share a SLIP connection (serial line internet protocol)	$60 per month
Medium-sized company, up to 30 employees	UUCP (UNIX to UNIX Copy)	$60 per month
Medium to large company	Dedicated 56-Kbps, ISDN or frame-relay connections	$3600–$7500 per year provides a dedicated line, unlimited access
Large corporation	Dedicated T1 line	$15,000 annually

Many companies are reluctant to use this strategic weapon because of concerns over security. Recently, there have been publicized reports of security breaches, viruses and crashes on the Internet. During a House Subcommittee on Science hearing, the manager of the federally funded Computer Emergency Response Team (CERT) told House members that after a systemwide security breach, 27 sites discovered monitoring programs, which intercept user passwords, installed on their computers. This type of publicity does not comfort companies that want to keep their communications private. In fact, according to a survey conducted by the Electronic Messaging Association, only 4% of the sites surveyed use only a public e-mail system, and 71% of sites use a private e-mail system exclusively (see Figure 4-4).

From a technology standpoint, however, there is no reason why companies can't encrypt electronic mail or data for greater security. Data communications on the Internet is only as insecure as the encryption techniques that are used and the people who handle the data. CERT also recommends that users employ non-reusable passwords.

By setting up their own host (a node), a company can further control security considerations, including access; the information that comes in and out; e-mail and the amount and types of news distributed. From a data communications standpoint, it is difficult to control connections to this enormous public data network. And, for financial transactions, the Internet would not be a good medium because there is no guaranteed delivery, and certain things, such as server downtime, are not in the control of one company. However, by owning a host, a company can limit the disadvantages of being connected to the public network.

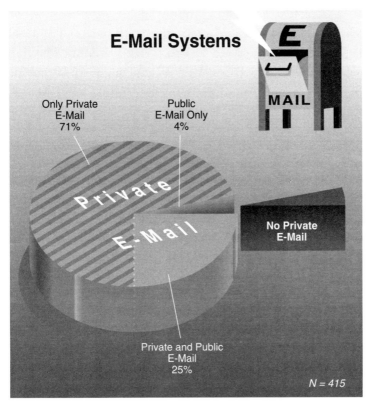

Figure 4–4 Private e-mail systems dominate for both headquarter and branch sites. More than 90% of the sites surveyed in a study have a private e-mail system. (Courtesy Electronic Messaging Association)

The communication capabilities of the SuperNet have created new business opportunities for companies throughout Colorado. The Colorado Department of Purchasing is planning to use the Internet to disseminate information about what is out for bid. This service enhances the ability of small business throughout the state to respond to requests for proposals (RFPs).

Entire towns are now gearing up to go on-line. Along with five other rural Colorado communities and coalitions, the Steamboat Springs and Yampa Valley Economic Development Councils jointly received a state grant that provides funding to use telecommunications for creating jobs, strengthening schools, providing health care and creating community electronic town halls.

"We have always been a relatively isolated area geographically," notes Linda Kakela, city grants coordinator for the city of Steamboat Springs. "With upgrades in our regional jetport and telecommunications infrastructure we can compete with metro areas, attracting a substantial number of lone eagles, people who will be telecommuting to their businesses."

The Internet is not the only information highway that companies and individuals use to connect with each other. Indeed, there are many highways and services, owned and operated by a variety of players (see Table 4-2).

Table 4-2   Information Highway Access

Information Highway Players	Examples of Companies
Individual companies	Numerous
Local telephone companies	Numerous
Long-distance carriers	AT&T, MCI, Sprint
The seven regional Bell operating companies (RBOCs)	Ameritech, Bell Atlantic, BellSouth, Nynex, Pacific Telesis, Southwestern Bell, US West
Cable system operators	Continental Cablevision, Jones Intercable, Tele-Communications, Inc.

Table 4-2   Information Highway Access (Continued)

Information Highway Players	Examples of Companies
Wireless communications	Ardis, CDPD, Nextel Communications, Nationwide Wireless Network, Metricom, Orbcomm, Ram Mobile Data
Network technology and service providers	Advantis (Sears and IBM partnership)
Information service providers	Dow-Jones, Time Warner

As the connections between the highways become more seamless and as the on- and off-ramps or gateways that connect individual businesses, schools and homes to the highway are developed, the applications and benefits of this electronic medium will bloom. An article by Andy Reinhardt in *BYTE* magazine elaborates:

"For business users, the data highway represents the holy grail of connectivity: a ubiquitous internetwork that allows them easily and inexpensively to connect with customers and suppliers, improve communications among employees, and gather competitive data. Applications facilitated by the highway, such as videoconferencing, document sharing, and multimedia e-mail, could reduce travel spending and encourage telecommuting. Businesses might also save big on reduced healthcare costs if the data highway improves distribution of medical records and enable new techniques such as remote diagnostics."[1]

---

1. Reinhardt, Andy, "Building the Data Highway," *Byte*, March 1994, p. 46.

Keeping on Top of the Rumor Mill

The speed at which electronic communications travel makes it important for corporate communicators to respond rapidly to events that may tie up the computer network. The technology eliminates lead time on internal stories or issues. With a short lead time between stories, rumors occur more easily and run rampant faster than they do in non-electronic environments. Communicators must be able to produce and distribute information faster than rumors circulate on the grapevine.

An incident on the Internet illustrates the power of the electronic grapevine. Several years ago, someone got on a bulletin board system (BBS) and 'talked' about date rape. Once that message got on the Internet, it got into about 3-1/2 million different computers. Almost 2-1/2 million users, both male and female, wrote back to express their opinions. The system got to the point where it could hardly move. If the president of a company is in fast communications, electronic communications, with everyone on the staff, and he or she makes a controversial statement, the organization will be paralyzed with responses. One of the important roles of corporate communications is to sort the wheat from the chaff.

Randall Whiting of Hewlett-Packard suggests that the technology becomes dysfunctional when communication that is intended to have a limited distribution suddenly gets out of control. He says, "We have an electronic conferencing system that was designed to allow ongoing conversations on-line between research and development engineers. They can have an ongoing discussion on the system where someone writes: 'I am using this new component and I'm running into a problem. Here are the needs that I have and here is our approach. Has anybody come up with a way to improve our yield on this or the performance?' Six engineers may contribute ideas electronically to the original question. There is great benefit in sharing information like that.

"The problem that arises for internal communications is that information intended for dissemination on a very limited basis becomes available throughout the company much more quickly electronically. It makes it easy for somebody in Massachusetts who hears a rumor about a new product, division or layoffs to put that out on the conference system and ask, 'Who knows what's going on here?' Suddenly employees in California and Colorado are asking about it. So internal communicators have an enormous burden to be able to stay on top of rumor control and manage a short lead time on the announcement of changes."

Whiting also recommends that communications professionals make senior executives aware of the implications of communicating electronically. He says, "In this environment access to information is much easier. The fundamental nature of corporate communications changes because you have to work within the technology infrastructure. Technology increases the velocity of the information as it travels through the company. Instead of becoming an information gatekeeper you manage the flow, adjust the valves at different spots. You also have to be a close consultant to management because management has to understand the state of information flow within the company. It becomes incumbent upon the internal communications people to tell management, 'If you make this announcement, here is the implication, not only in Omaha, but in Chicago, Boston and Miami.' "

Filtering Prevents Overload

Communicators also need to prevent the confusion that occurs with information overload. With approximately 2,500 offices in 140 countries, American Express places great emphasis on effectively communicating with employees. Former Vice President of Corporate Employee Communications Ron Martin believes the communications department must take an active role in ensuring that electronic communications remain a valuable service for employees. "One of my concerns is communication clutter," he says. "As more of this technology comes on board and companies start using it, it places some burden on people in corporate communications to make policy decisions and exercise control over access to these communication channels. At American Express we worked to cut down the quantity of publications and paper that cross our employees' desks because otherwise they cease to be effective. It's like junk mail at home. We are on the verge of that on the electronic side if we don't put some restrictions on access to electronic channels."

To prevent information clutter, American Express developed policies to control the quantity of information that goes out to employees. These policies cover print and electronic communications. Martin explains, "Everybody liked to go out and create a newsletter. Newsletters were proliferating. We said that any employee should receive no more than three publications…one from the corporate parent, one from the business unit and one that might be strictly local in nature. Everything should be channeled into those three publications. It then became critical to develop policies as the use and awareness of electronic messaging increased."

In a large organization it is impossible to filter all of the information placed on a network. Martin Nisenholtz, Senior

Vice President at Ogilvy and Mather Direct, suggests that filtering should depend upon the application. He argues that if applications are broken into different categories, certain applications require a gatekeeping function, and others don't. For example, you don't have a gatekeeping function when an employee sends an electronic memo to somebody, but you do have a gatekeeping function when the chairman sends a memo to the staff.

Nisenholtz goes on to explain that the old motto of "quality not quantity" holds true for electronic communications: "One of the most important issues is the quality of the information itself, not whether somebody gets what they want or don't want. The fact is that while there is a lot of information overload, which to some extent spills over into meeting overload, much of it is junk. I think these networks have to be filters and junk eliminators. People have to make qualitative judgments about the information itself. I'm trying to provide distribution. I can't guarantee that once I do that, anything is going to happen other than more information overload. I would hope the enhanced distribution, and the software that allows you to filter provide mechanisms for people to act intelligently."

The issues of overload and security are critical in the financial industry. The volume of information is tremendous, and the information is sensitive. Merrill Lynchs' Rich Gaiti elaborates: "Information comes from many different sources. It can come from corporate communications, administration, operations—or sources external to the firm. There is not one single source of information, nor has there ever been. We are trying to take all the multiple sources that we have and filter them into one delivery vehicle. Because we are an information-based firm, there are different gatekeepers for different reasons. From the information services point of view, we like to have users be responsible for the quality and quantity of the information. They should be gatekeepers and editors."

At Merrill Lynch the computer system itself helps direct and secure the information. Gaiti explains, "We have a good security system. It ensures that people look at appropriate information. It also helps us understand who is at the workstation and how we should be able to direct pertinent information to that individual. We use the electronic security system as both gatekeeper and traffic cop."

Richard Levine of Dow Jones Information Services says, "An information-rich company, where hundreds or thousands of employees have direct access to information, is a company that in the long term will function more efficiently. Many companies use central collection points for information. Increasingly, we see the desire to spread information throughout the corporation. The needs of employees in different parts of the company, whether geographic or departmental, are very different. If the systems are well designed, then individual users can become their own gatekeepers. They can tailor the system to get what they need."

Information Security—Is It Possible?

Security is a major concern on interconnected networks where potentially thousands of people communicate with each other. There are several concerns:

1. Who has access to what?

2. Will the network accurately deliver the information from point A to point B?

3. Will it be possible to trace the trail of electronic information as it flows through an organization?

4. What are the legal ramifications of sending electronic information?

In an article in *Technology Review,* Michael Dertouzos describes features that should be required for a National Information Infrastructure, a network that would allow computer users throughout the United States to communicate easily with each other. One area of concern is the ability of the telecommunications lines to accurately transmit the data. He writes:

> "Shipping photographs of wheat fields from across the nation to a server computer that forecasts total wheat production could be effective even if a small portion of the data representing these pictures (say, less than 1 percent) were lost. Such an error, however, would be devastating in transmitting financial data, software, or circuit diagrams. Today, the telephone companies do offer special, cleaner lines, yet people who wish to ensure totally noise-free transmissions must keep resending and checking data on their own until it is faithfully received."[2]

The ability to ensure privacy for communications is also important. Certain types of communication, such as legal contracts or new product designs need to be scrambled to ensure privacy. Federal Express believes privacy is important for information distributed to large audiences. They secure the FXTV video network with an encryption system, and place the audio portion of the program on a secure 700-line that can only be accessed from a Federal Express facility.

---

2. Michael L. Detouzos, "Building the Information Marketplace," *Technology Review,* January 1991, p. 32.

In a large, decentralized organization employees from many different departments may be placing information onto the network. To achieve security, organizations must limit the number of people who can create or alter electronic documents. Passwords for authors ensure that other employees cannot tamper with documents.

Two approaches can be taken with respect to employees who read electronic documents. The first approach assumes that the audience for on-line documents encompasses all LAN- and WAN-connected employees. Any employee with a computer attached to a local area network will be able to receive the communications. Proprietary information and confidential documents are not distributed. There are several positive aspects to this approach. It establishes a framework whereby all employees are considered equal with respect to information. It opens an organization with respect to sharing nonconfidential documents, such as human resource policies, benefits information and company news. This can be extremely healthy for an organization, increasing dialogue between different departments, employees and management.

A second approach assumes that only designated employees will be able to receive information. This may be necessary with respect to sales or budget information, customer profiles or product distribution data targeted to specific managers. Secure telecommunications lines, encryption of information and computer passwords can provide control over the accuracy and privacy of communications.

Legal issues also arise with electronic communication. In the past, a paper trail provided security by archiving the internal flow of communication. An electronic trail can be maintained, but it may require too much system memory to be effective. Discussing the security of electronic communications, Larry Prusak of Ernst & Young says, "Before you had electronic mail or information technology, memos were done on paper. People would save documents because they showed the trail, and with litigation you want to examine how a decision was made. For a number of reasons record management occurred. With electronic mail, people send messages back and forth on a terminal, and messages aren't saved. You cannot really find the paper trail."

Bernard Mathaisel, also with Ernst & Young, suggests that technology can help: "Record-keeping can be addressed with the technology. Many electronic mail systems keep archival copies of all documents. Not only can you keep the result of the event, you can track the formation of events, the aftermath and everything along the way. You may want to investigate how it occurred, and why it occurred. However, if we start saving, tracking individual actions right on down to the keystroke level, then we will absolutely explode the stuff that we must keep."

Besides hindering productivity, this type of detailed technological tracking raises issues of individual privacy. Organizations must develop policies with respect to the ability of managers or departments (such as security) to record or monitor the electronic communications that take place between individuals.

Electronic Information: Here Comes the Judge

Arthur Cordell, an advisor on information technology policy for the Canadian Department of Communications, points out that computer-based communications allow readers to make editorial decisions. He writes: "The new media are interactive. This stands in contrast to all previous media, where the product was a single package whose content and format was controlled by editors. Now, the new media permit the user rather than the publisher to select the style, organization, order, and content of the items."[3]

The technology not only allows users to decide what they want to see and read, but the order and fashion in which they see and read it. This raises the issue of whether communicators maintain responsibility for the comprehension or use of the material. The burden of legal liability related to electronically stored documents is another issue. Discussing concerns related to tampering with electronic documentation, Tony Van Atta, Program Manager for Documentation Information Services at Northern Telecom, says, "We ran into this issue with our attorneys when we were first doing our documents. Initially, we had the capability for people to take ASCII text and access the document in that format. At that time, our legal opinion was to disable the function. If someone takes one of our documents and revises it, and something happens to it, we could be technically liable because they have altered the document. The issue came back that as long as we have our original file on a CD-ROM disk that cannot be changed, we can prove in a court of law that somebody changed it."

The issue of liability with respect to text revision becomes increasingly important as organizations begin to use a document transfer standard know, as Standardized Generalized Markup Language (SGML). SGML grew out of a Department of Defense initiative. The standard allows users who have different software to effectively share files without losing the visual appearance and formatting of the document. Formatting incudes attributes such as typefaces, underlining, boldface, indentations and headings. Using SGML, documents are tagged in a specific way. One tag may represent a chapter title; another

---

3. Arthur J. Cordell, *The Futurist,* March-April 1991, p. 21.

may represent text body with certain attributes. This standard ensures that as documents are transmitted from sender to receiver, there are no changes in appearance.

Van Atta believes that SGML creates certain risks regarding information security. He says, "One issue relates to the fact that SGML is a revisable text file. What happens if I give you my file, and on page 57 there is a red label that says, 'WARNING if you unplug this system Florida is going to lose voice messaging,' and you reformat that so the warning exists on another page? I'm sorry, but I'm not liable for that. That is the revision issue. Our position is, if you get our documentation in a revisable format, the warranty is void at this time unless you can prove in a court of law that you have procedures in place, controls that guarantee the document will never be changed."

In addition to concerns about what customers may do with information, organizations must also consider issues of copyright, ownership and royalty fees when distributing documents to internal audiences. If information is taken from a document that has a copyright, or is delivered by an electronic wireservice that owns a copyright, it may be necessary to pay fees prior to redistribution. The copyright law provides publishers a variety of rights under Title 17 of the United States code. These include the right of reproduction, the right of distribution, the right of public display, the right of public performance and the right to create derivative works.

When the copyright law was revised in 1978, Congress recommended the establishment of a photocopy licensing mechanism such as the Copyright Clearance Center (CCC). A consortium of rightsholders, including the Association of American Publishers, The Authors League of America and the Information Industry Association, along with users of copyrighted material, helped organize this not-for-profit entity. The CCC helps organizations manage copyright concerns and licensing fees. It conveys licenses or permissions to use copyrighted information to users, and royalties to the rightsholders. The CCC has approximately 4,500 corporations and subsidiaries under license in the photocopy domain.

Today, in addition to authorizing organizations to photocopy materials, the CCC offers a license for digital use of full text in networked environments within a corporate setting. These collective licenses are positioned to transcend rapidly evolving technology by authorizing a "faithful and accurate reproduction" of material on internal networks. Only users authorized by the licensee may access material, which is safeguarded by systems features such as metering, and by contractual understandings between the Licensee and the CCC on behalf of its rightsholders.

Joseph Alen, President and CEO of the Copyright Clearance Center, explains how copyright law impacts electronic communications. "The law provides clear and explicit requirements for the utilization of copyrighted materials," he says. "For example, the entry of a work into a computer system via scanning or distribution on a network of a copyrighted item requires the permission of the rightsholder under most circumstances. If you translate a work into a machine language, that act relates to the right of creation of a derivative work. Or, if you call up an item on a screen from a system, that is considered the exercise of a display right. In many instances, the rightsholder requests a royalty fee for any of these uses of that material."

In the digital environment as well as in the photocopying domain, it would be difficult, if not impossible, for an organization to get license agreements for use of material with copyright from all of the different rightsholders. In fact, there are millions of rightsholders, titles and end users. A collective organization like the CCC in the United States, and through bilateral relations with counterpart organizations overseas, forms a network that can grant authorizations and collect royalties.

The Copyright Clearance Center is unique because it relies on voluntary contractual relationships with rightsholders—principally publishers—rather than any form of legal statute to build its repertory. Publishers have traditionally been concerned with the extent of the rights transferred from their authors, control of their material and pricing. In the digital environment, there is also greater concern about loss of subscriptions. Despite these obstacles, the CCC now licenses photocopying from the works of more than 4,000 publishers in the United States and more than 8,600 worldwide.

From an initial venture into electronic licensing on a limited pilot basis (started in 1990), CCC has expanded into a full collective licensing system for digital uses. The fundamental principle of rightsholder price setting remains the same. Unlike compulsory licensing schemes in Europe and Asia, the CCC approach remains voluntary, with control remaining vested in the rightsholder.

Currently available only to commercial corporations, and representing a substantially smaller repertory than the photocopy license, the digital use license will "authorize the full panoply of copyright utilization," according to Alen. "What is not permitted is any commercial exploitation or moving material out into larger network systems. So, in the case of a corporation, agreements are for use within the corporation. They couldn't put the material out through the Internet to another corporation." The license is also flexible as to the source of information, covering both material provided by the publisher in electronic form as well as electronic information converted from print by the end user.

"We anticipate that collective licenses in the electronic environment will reflect differences from the photocopy licenses that are driven by the medium itself," says Alen. "Though users will still seek a range of materials, each user will be interested in a unique mix of critical materials. The CCC can provide that access and assemble the electronic rights for those products. The pricing model developed balances the publisher's need for a return on these licenses and the users' concern with fair and predictable licensing systems. Publishers will set prices both for access and for individual transactions; users can then choose how they will structure their license, and therefore their price. Moreover, we will be more actively involved in a monitoring and oversight role for these licenses."

Organizations should also develop an internal policy statement regarding the distribution of electronic information. This document has several objectives. It establishes guidelines for the visual style of electronic documents, thereby creating a consistent look and feel to electronic documents that will prevent readers from being confused when they connect to different documents. It protects the organization from legal and security problems that may arise from the distribution of proprietary material. It defines for document authors the type of material that is suitable for electronic distribution. And it specifies the technical and administrative procedures that provide electronic security to the system. Input on the policy statement should come from four areas of an organization: corporate communications, legal, security and information systems. Table 4-3 lists some of the input and responsibilities for these departments.

Table 4-3   Gatekeeping Policy Statement

I. Communications

Consults with different departments that need to distribute documents. Addresses issues related to suitability of information distribution such as audience size, departments and public affairs issues (if the general public will see the information). Sets guidelines with respect to the visual appearance of information, the style of documents, use of color and company logos.

II. Legal

Address issues related to electronic distribution of copyright information. Makes policy limiting distribution of information that customers receive.

III. Security

Makes policy regarding issue of distribution of confidential and restricted company information.

IV. Information Services

Develops security for access to authors who put information on the system and access to readers. Develops batch files to monitor the usage of the system.

A gatekeeping policy statement will help different departments in an organization understand their responsibilities with respect to electronic communications.

As the quantity of available information continues to swell and it becomes increasingly easy to communicate with personal computers, the role for the corporate communications department changes from information provider to information manager and consultant. This new role requires new skills for communication professionals. Communicators must understand the technology and comprehend the impact that instantaneous communications can have on employees in a decentralized environment. Issues relating to privacy, security, legal liability and copyright must be addressed as computer networks become widely used for internal and external communication.

Talk Back to Me:
Two Way Communications

The technology of the computer allows us to have
a distinct and individually tailored arrangement
with each of thousands of employees.

—John Naisbitt, Megatrends,
(Warner Books)

Interactive, two-way communications. It is a skill we
begin to develop at birth, and one we continue to use daily in
life and business. Communication technology ultimately suc-
ceeds when it enhances dialogue between individuals. That is
why the telephone, CB, ham and broadcast radio and videoconferencing have flourished. Now, with network connection,
desktop computers open new vistas in interactive communication. No longer are messages sent into a black hole where it is
never really clear what employees think about the messages, or
worse, whether they even receive them. With electronic communications, surveys of employee attitudes can be taken
instantaneously. Information can be shared on electronic bul-

letin boards, and multiple users can simultaneously work on documents. Two-way communications via computer offers users benefits that have not previously been available. These benefits can significantly improve organizational efficiency.

Two-Way Is Better than One-Way

As organizations evolve and grow, the nature of internal communication changes. The larger an organization becomes, the more difficult it is to get feedback from employees. At the beginning of an organization's life cycle, communication starts with face-to-face interaction. As organizations grow, they displace face-to-face meetings with other methods of communication. This includes print, audio-visual, telephone and now computers.

The PC network really becomes a lifeline for both sending information out to employees and getting feedback. Brian White is the Director of Employee Communications at GTE Telephone Operations. White believes that using networks for interactive communications is a critical element in business strategy. He says, "It can do nothing but help communications in companies. Most of the research that we have conducted shows that employees want to be able to hear company direction directly from management. When you are talking about Fortune 100 companies, that often means management in another state or city. Videoconferencing and electronic mail provide a means for employees to get that information directly from the people they want to hear it from, the people that lead the company. It also gives employees a means to provide feedback on company issues, and ask questions about company direction."

Beyond providing a forum for discussion about important company issues, feedback on the network can be used for sales, marketing or public relations activities. Sue Cushing at

MCI provides an example: "If a competitor has an outage, I can send out a message saying, 'Have any of our customers called? Have they switched services, or bought more MCI services because of the outage?' I may be asking these questions because we've received a media inquiry. I get information back very quickly."

Taking the Pulse of an Organization with Electronic Surveys

Bruce McKenzie, President of Business Information Graphics, consults with companies that use their computer networks to communicate with employees. McKenzie admits that the networks are not usually created with the intention of being a channel for communications. "The network is probably put in for other purposes," he notes. "It is put in to transmit huge amounts of data or graphics, not for employee communications. The networks are, or will, be there. The challenge is what do you do with them besides send spreadsheets. You can use those networks to deliver corporate information to involve employees in communications that are interactive, conversational, informal and offer instant access. It is a different communication medium from anything that is printed."

McKenzie is a strong believer in using the two-way nature of the networks. "The most important thing is allowing employees to respond. It's like, 'Oh I got this survey on my computer screen, and they want my feedback. I click this button or type my comments in this box, and they go back to the people that are gathering the information.' This gives communicators a method of conducting ongoing employee surveys. It provides a constant feedback mechanism."

Feedback from employees has been a tradition at IBM. IBM launched its renowned Speak Up program in 1959 as a method for employees to anonymously address questions and concerns to upper management. Since its introduction, the program has generated more than 300,000 comments from employees around the world. Following this tradition, IBM uses on-line surveys to periodically take the pulse of the company.

Andy McCormick, an IBM spokesperson, says, "We do an employee opinion survey which is about 25 years old now. IBM employees will take an opinion survey every 12 to 18 months. It is a series of 60 to 80 questions. Some change, and some remain the same over the years. It occurs on-line, anonymously. Questions are about everything from immediate management to 'Do you like the direction the company as a whole has taken?'"

The results of these electronic surveys are given to a manager, who then holds a meeting two or three weeks after the survey. He or she discusses the results and develops an action plan to change or correct areas of concern. Then managers are measured, last year against the current year, when employees take the survey again.

McCormack believes the feedback helps IBM understand how employees perceive their message, and identifies issues that are important to various audiences. He says, "We can really measure changes in attitudes and opinions. When the company is trying new things or putting in new programs, it is quite easy to see what is getting through to people, what they feel is important and not important. That ultimately contributes to the bottom line."

Merrill Lynch uses on-line surveys to improve communications and marketing. "We are putting in an automatic survey system on our workstations," explains Ritch Gaiti. "The marketing department will use this to supplement what they normally do. We frequently survey our people to understand what they are thinking, what their clients are thinking. This automated version should enable us to do that a lot faster, and do some 'real-time' surveying. For example, as we're doing a direct broadcast to offices and talking about some issue, we might ask them to come back into us or respond via the survey system and give us their thoughts on the issues. So we force faster, high-quality, structured, two-way communications."

Sharing Thoughts with Groupware

Letting employees connect simultaneously to computer applications is a logical extension of the technology. The network already connects everyone. Why not communicate in real time? Most people are familiar with audio teleconferences, where several individuals at different locations share a conversation on the telephone. Connecting simultaneously via computer offers some unique communications capabilities.

Groupware encompasses programs that allow two or more users to work on a project independently or simultaneously. The single biggest advantage of groupware is its ability to improve communications, thereby speeding up development of a project. Group authoring is one application for groupware. With group authoring, a document is electronically shared among various authors for review and changes. Depending upon the software, there are two approaches for groupware authoring. In one approach, an author writes the document and then electronically shares it with reviewers, who add their input or make revisions when it is convenient. The software automatically collates all suggestions, highlighting them next to the original text. The author and reviewers can see each other's remarks. The process saves a tremendous amount of time because the author can focus attention on evaluating comments made by reviewers rather than managing a trail of paper.

The second approach to groupware authoring is software that allows the author(s) and reviewers to work simultaneously on a document. This is similar to a conference call where the PC screen becomes a work area for people attending the conference. Sometimes, users find it advantageous to use both a telephone connection and the PC connection so they can simultaneously talk about and share suggestions. Table 5-1 compares features of several groupware products.

Table 5-1   Groupware Products

Product Name	How It Works
Aspect Group Logic	Users can work on a document simultaneously
For Comment Computer Associates	Users can make comments which are shared among the group
Lotus Notes Lotus Development	Users can schedule meetings, track projects and exchange information

Groupware software allows users to share, review and modify documents, either simultaneously or at whatever time is convenient.

Groupware improves meetings by eliminating personality conflicts that stifle or reduce productivity. Scott Johnson, President of NTERGAID, a software company based in Fairfield, Connecticut, considers groupware meetings to be superior to old-fashioned sit-downs. He says, "In most meetings you've got one person talking, five sleeping or doodling and two participating. Or, everybody's participating and nobody is paying attention. All of the seminal groupware research shows that when you use a computer you eliminate the personal factor in terms of relationships. Multimedia brings back the personal factor without the overhead of relationship friction. That help individuals communicate better."

Groupware even improves productivity at companies that produce software. Based in Redmond, Washington, Microsoft Corporation is the leading developer of personal computer systems and applications software in the world, and Chairman and CEO Bill Gates is one of the richest men in the world, with an estimated personal fortune of $7 billion. Annual company sales have skyrocketed from $346 million in 1987 to more than $2 billion today. MS-DOS, Microsoft's operating system software, runs on approximately 81% of the 22 million IBM-compatible PCs manufactured each year. Windows, the company's graphical interface software, is no small success either, selling about one million copies every month. Microsoft will continue to be a major player in the information revolution as it creates software that enables the digital convergence of computers, phones and electronics.

Microsoft University is Microsoft's education and consulting group. The charter of the University is to work with the Microsoft product line and establish a presence in the computer industry in terms of training and education for external customers. Mark Protus, Manager of Media Production at Microsoft University, believes groupware has inherent pros and cons. "The positive side is that the technology allows for quick communication. When you get several people online, you operate in a fashion that involves a lot of ideas and opinions," he says. As for his own experience, "Groupware is interesting. I create multimedia. When we work with teams that have unique talents, where people use information in different ways, it is a great way to schedule information to ensure that everyone has the most up-to-date information. Everybody in a team follows a project together. If you need to communicate quickly two or three people talk at the same time."

Protus acknowledges that without visuals and sound, communications via computer challenges the normal process of discussion. "The flip side of the technology is that you can't read expressions on e-mail. You can't get hints of intonation or inflection that come about with normal communication," he says. "When you're dealing with design and creative issues, often listening to somebody's intonation or seeing the expression on their face works better. Also, the skill sets that you use interpersonally don't always translate electronically. Somebody who can wow a crowd in person might be a terrible speller, and the message they convey comes out differently electronically. Electronic communication is a different way of presenting yourself. But group communication is just starting. Perhaps there is a different paradigm to using electronic group communication than there is to brainstorming with everyone in one room."

Workflow Applications: Helping Information Move Through the Company

When it comes to software applications, there is always another plateau, another generation that offers more benefits, more features. Workflow applications represent the latest development in software. Groupware allows individuals who are geographically separated, but are usually in the same department or organization, to share and update thoughts. Workflow applications go one step further, enabling documents, mail, files and forms to be routed automatically through various departments and organizations in a company.

With workflow, an insurance claim form would move effortlessly from the initial claims office through adjustors all the way through final payment via networks. All forms, signatures, even photographic images would be clipped together electronically. If the client calls in to request an update, customer service can quickly access the file and report the status without a long, delayed search. In addition to improving customer satisfaction with the process, workflow applications can save tremendous sums of money with respect to improving efficiency, enhancing cross-functional communication, tracking and maintaining accurate files and reducing paperwork.

Workflow also provides companies with a competitive advantage in the marketplace. By connecting research and development, engineering, manufacturing and sales and marketing organizations during the development and introduction of new products, workflow technology enhances speed-to-market. Simultaneous or concurrent engineering refers to the process whereby these different organizations share product design, manufacturing and marketing ideas electronically as a product is developed. For example, computer-aided design and manufacturing schematics can be routed electronically for discussion.

The significant benefit is that any changes in design that may be required as a product goes from initial concept through manufacturing and, finally, sales will now be determined up front—before changes involve costly retooling of manufacturing operations or rethinking of marketing plans. Competition is fierce in the global economy of the 1990s. Companies cannot afford lengthy design, engineering or marketing time frames with respect to product development. In addition, product life cycles continue to decrease as new products are brought to market faster. By using workflow applications as part of the simultaneous engineering process, companies can reduce product development time by more than 50%. As a result, the company saves money in the development process and establishes a competitive edge over competitors.

The implementation of workflow applications continues to accelerate as the number of local and wide area networks increases and powerful PCs find their way to more desktops. One important subset of workflow applications is the "electronic form." Electronic forms are themselves created by software programs. On the most basic level, electronic forms simply duplicate an organizational document that needs to be shuffled from one person to another. More advanced electronic forms have fields that are linked directly to databases of information. Sophisticated software and forms have routing routines that move the form from one person to another automatically. Table 5-2 shows a few of the workflow and electronic form applications that are available today.

Table 5-2   Workflow and Electronic Forms Software

Company	Product	Category
BeyondMail	Forms Designer	Electronic form
Delrina Corp.	Delrina FormFlow	Electronic form
FileNet Corporation	Workflow	Workflow
IBM Corp.	FlowMark	Workflow
IBM Corp.	FormTalk	Electronic form
JetForm Corp	JetForm	Electronic form
Microsoft Corp.	Electronic Forms Designer	Electronic form
Sigma Imaging	Omnidesk	Workflow

**Table 5-2   Workflow and Electronic Forms
Software (Continued)**

Company	Product	Category
ViewStar	Workbench	Workflow
WordPerfect Corp.	WordPerfect InForms	Electronic form

As applications increase, more companies offer workflow and electronic forms software.

Electronic Bulletin Boards
Don't Require Thumbtacks

Electronic bulletin board systems (BBS) represent yet
another vehicle for interaction between employees, or between
companies and their customers. "Bulletin board system" is
really a generic term which has come to encompass most electronic systems that users can dial into with a modem. There
are a variety of bulletin boards and applications, including special topic bulletin boards, shareware file libraries, real-time
chat functions and purely informational systems. Bulletin
boards can be used by either small or broad groups of people.
Unlike groupware, which is designed to help users complete
specific projects with deadlines, bulletin boards are usually
open-ended. Private companies now operate approximately
130,000 electronic bulletin boards. There are three main
applications:

1. Internal communications via e-mail

2. Customer service and support via dial-in

3. Direct sales to customers

The most popular use of bulletin boards for business
applications is as an internal communications medium. For a

few thousand dollars, a company can put up a system that could provide electronic mail, possibly on-line inventory or a product directory.

There are shareware bulletin board software packages that can be registered for as little as $50. All that is required is a PC, a modem and a telephone line. For less than $1,000 a small company can install a very basic system. A comprehensive eight-line system can cost less than $10,000.

With readers in 60 countries, *Boardwatch Magazine* is the leading publication for bulletin board users. Jack Rickard, Editor and Publisher of *Boardwatch*, discusses the use of bulletin boards for customer service and direct sales. "One area that works extremely well is for high-technology companies where the client base will have modems," he says. "Numerous software and hardware companies offer product support and technical support on bulletin board systems because 90% of the calls from their customers will focus on the same 'top ten' questions. So, these companies enhance customer service by posting the questions and answers on a bulletin board system. This is less expensive than paying someone to answer calls. It is also more convenient for customers because problems can occur at 9:00 p.m. When there is no one to call, they can simply dial in."

Another growing area is the use of bulletin boards as a direct on-line sales tool. Customers can connect, select items from inventory, pay with a credit card and the products are delivered to their doorstep. "This application is used mostly by direct mail or direct marketing companies," explains Rickard. "Tower Records, for example, might have 13,000 titles of compact audio disks in a store. The bulletin board has a database of 52,000 disks, and users can search for them in very convenient ways. The company uses a drop ship arrangement with distributors that deliver to the customer's home."

At IBM, video announcements on the company's internal television network encourage employees to access bulletin boards. As employees walk down the hallway, they see a video monitor displaying a short 10 second headline that reads, 'See your bulletin board.' Employees may be intrigued by that and go enter the bulletin board to call up the full text of the announcement. IBM is a large company with different things going on, and it's not always easy to keep track of what new products are coming out. Although the focus of bulletin boards is on different business groups, divisions and technology groups might oversee one. IBM operates numerous bulletin boards, but there are a few that are company-wide which most employees receive.

The ability to network with other employees and receive help on a project is extremely powerful. Bruce McKenzie of Business Information Graphics agrees that bulletin boards dramatically improve productivity. Stressing the importance of creativity, McKenzie provides an example of a application for bulletin boards. He says, "Everyone involved in energy conservation in a big manufacturing company could have their own bulletin board, or two-way communications system, like an internal Internet. This is a vastly superior alternative to what often occurs when a company goes on a crusade for cost management, or energy conservation, or resource recovery. Typically, somebody gets put in charge of the function, holds a conference, sends out a newsletter or otherwise tries to drum up interest in the project where he or she has very little direct influence over employees. If you set up an electronic system, you create something more involving than a newsletter…perhaps a contest or a game."

Industry associations and information providers are rapidly jumping on this bandwagon to provide electronic information to members and professionals. In fact, you can find information about any subject that impacts business and industry. The Society for Manufacturing Engineers (SME), for example, operates a bulletin board system that provides members an opportunity to share information and download articles and files. Likewise, the National Association of Manufacturers (NAM) operates NAMnet. This public policy electronic network provides users access to the latest information concerning legislative and regulatory developments that impact companies, details about activities in the administration and Congress, congressional voting records, state issues and public policy information from a variety of organizations. And, if you need even more information about products and companies that impact industry, turn to *IndustryNet,* an on-line service created by Automation News Network for executives, engineering professionals and purchasing managers. *IndustryNet* provides e-mail, news and new product announcements, listings of used equipment and computers, a shareware library of more than 1,000 programs, a career opportunities section and stock indexes of emerging and growth companies providing engineering and manufacturing products. This service also has a connection to the Internet for broad distribution.

One of the problems that large organizations face with trying to share ideas, work on problems or simply store information is that size and geographical separation make it difficult, if not impossible, for an individual to know where to refer a question, or who is responsible for storing the knowledge he or she has accumulated. Usually, when faced with this barrier, employees simply give up. A standardized electronic communication system makes it possible, if not easy, for people to share their knowledge and information.

Arthur Andersen's Eric Dean agrees: "We have always operated as one firm worldwide for the purpose of pooling our knowledge. Now we have a tool that makes it practical to do that on a level that hasn't been possible before. There is the potential for automating a large set of processes which today require either someone to physically go somewhere or require a piece of paper to be manipulated.

"Often, however, the person who is a source of information may not know who is responsible for keeping track of the information; nor do they know how to get it to them. So a cataloger has a terrible job. Arthur Andersen, and other companies, by using a standardized, ubiquitous software package to create a medium where information and data is always in the same format, can build on that platform to also make the information easy to locate. This will help create a common interest in contributing to the electronic repository."

The personal computer is the perfect two-way communications medium. Like the telephone, the PC is rapidly becoming a common tool in most offices; but the PC has advantages over the telephone. Computers can simultaneously connect hundreds, even thousands, of employees and perform functions, such as tabulating survey responses and automatically highlighting revisions to text, which telephones cannot.

It is a good bet that the computer, once seen as a technological device which isolated workers, will enhance personal interaction between employees and help flatten organizational hierarchies that stifle growth and productivity. To take advantage of two-way interactive communications, organizations and individuals must be willing to develop creative approaches and applications for sharing information.

Multimedia Is Here to Stay

You cannot fight against the future.

—*William Edward Gladstone (1809–1898)*
Speech in Parliament

In addition to brains, the personal computer now has ears and eyes. Technologies that were recently worlds apart now converge on the workstation. Inexpensive audio boards and speakers provide audio-related applications such as voice messaging between computers. Electronic image capture systems allow users to scan and transmit visual copies of documents. Digital video promises instant access to video for training and communication. The ability of the workstation to combine different types of media, audio, video, graphics and text is appropriately referred to as multimedia. Multimedia offers users a superior communication and learning experience.

Video Is Hot!

If anyone has the audacity to suggest that television is not a powerful communication media, they need only be reminded that 98.2% of U.S. households own televisions, and the average viewer watches some 31 hours of programming per week.[1] The lure of video has not gone unnoticed by the business community, which now regularly uses television programming to deliver messages, enhance training and reduce the time and expense associated with travel.

Indeed, video has impact. Beyond receiving a message, viewers can see the visual cues presented by the person delivering the message, and listen to the inflection in their voice. As with text, video becomes more powerful when it offers two-way communication. With interactive videoconferencing, organizations increase the utility of television by allowing employees at different sites to see and talk to each other. Because it is interactive, videoconferencing can be used to conduct business meetings among people who are thousands of miles apart.

Video Distribution:
The Evolution Continues

There is a rapid and continuous evolution with respect to the distribution of video. Videoconferencing had its debut at the 1964 New York World's Fair. Unfortunately, high costs and expensive bandwidth requirements for the early systems prevented widespread application. For the business community, distribution of video in the 1960s involved mailing copies of videotapes to different sites. In the 1970s, large sites and corporate campuses began to use coaxial cable television net-

---

1. Television Bureau of Advertising Statistics.

Figure 6–1 Videoconferencing connects people. In the 1990s, videoconferencing is both flexible and affordable. Here, a fashion designer in Italy, reviews fabric with buyers in New York using the PictureTel System 1000. The desktop keypad (inset) controls visuals such as stored graphic images, moves the camera and adjusts audio. (Photo courtesy PictureTel)

works (also known as closed-circuit television, or CCTV) to send signals to employees at several locations. Two-way interactive applications involving remote locations grew with the installation of satellite uplink and downlink sites. This technology became readily available in the 1980s. Although initially expensive, applications involving multiple sites and numerous employees or managers could be cost justified. The pricing for a two-site satellite-based videoconference system continues to drop, from approximately $120,000 in 1985 to

Table 6-1 Videoconferencing Products

Company	Product	Platform	Compatibility	Bandwidth (kbit/s)	Price
ABL Engineering Menor, OH 216-974-8585	Interact	386, 486 PC	H.320, CIF	To 2 Mbit/s	$5,000
Intel Corp. Santa Clara, CA 800-538-3373	Proshare Video System 200	486 or Pentium	ISDN (Indeo)	128	$2,000
Northern Telecom Richardson, TX 800-NORTHERN	Visit Video	386, 486 PC Macintosh	H.320, ISDN QCIF	56 to 128	$3,000
PictureTel Danvers, MA 508-762-5000	PictureTel Live	386 and up	H.320, CIF ISDN, QCIF	56 to 384	$5,995
Silicon Graphics Mountain View, CA 800-800-7441	Indy Workstation	Indy	Proprietary	Ethernet LAN	$5,000
Vitel Corp. 117, 127 Austin, TX 800-284-8871	Vitel 115	386, 486 PC	ISDN, CIF, H.320	56 to 384	$14,900

$60,000 today. The cost of transmission via satellite is about $300 for a 30- to 60-minute program.

Technology continues to advance in the 1990s, allowing companies to transmit video signals over computer networks and even telephone lines. New applications integrate information from computers into the videoconference, allowing a group of people to watch and interact simultaneously with images of colleagues as well as computer files. Data on spreadsheets can be compared and instantly uploaded or downloaded from one site to another. Photographs of new products, engineering design schematics or financial charts can easily be reviewed and modified by managers at several locations. The final frontier in this technology allows individual users to conduct videoconferences via the computer in their office. Products that enable computers to conduct videoconferences sell for as low as $2,000. Equipment and computer chip manufacturers are pushing advances in technology that will create further price reductions. In one year, Intel will spend as much as $100 million on research, development and promotion of its videoconferencing products. Figure 6-1 shows videoconferencing in action. Table 6-1 contains information on various videoconferencing products.

Overcoming Challenges

There are three challenges to widespread distribution of video over computer and telephone networks. First, most telecommunications lines cannot carry the vast amount of information in a real-time video signal. One solution to this obstacle has been to compress the digital video signal before transmission. The receiving computer then decompresses the signal for viewing. The alternative to sending digitized video is to retrofit computers to accept analog video signals (regular

TV signals) that transmit on coaxial cable. This is the same type of cable that cable television operators use to transmit signals into television sets.

In the 1990s managers will witness an increasing use of both computer and telephone networks for distribution of interactive video. Technically, the capability to transmit video over telephone lines began in the early 1980s. At that time, codec (coder-decoder) manufacturers began to offer "black boxes" that compressed a normal video signal through a complex algorithm, enabling businesses and schools to receive signals in both video and audio format simultaneously in full-duplex (two-way) fashion. Initially, video codec manufacturers offered this solution via fiber optic transmission lines. These lines were, and continue to be, cost-prohibitive for long distance applications, especially to remote locations.

Other options that have become popular for transmission include leasing either a switched or dedicated digital network such as an integrated services digital network (ISDN). ISDN is a worldwide digital communications network that is emerging from existing telephone services and is designed to replace all current systems with a completely digital transmission system. Computers connect to ISDN via simple, standardized interfaces. ISDN broadband systems transmit voice, video, music and data.[2]

In addition to ISDN, in the late 1980s vendors began to offer devices that compress the video signal enough to transmit over copper telephone lines. Early versions could only transmit at 15 frames per second (the standard for full-motion video is 30 frames per second). Today, compression algorithms

---

2. ISDN consists of three communications channels: two B channels that transmit data at 64 kilobytes per second; and one D channel that carries information at 16 kilobytes per second.

exist that compress and transmit video at 30 frames per second, providing outstanding audio and video.

There is a simple equation that companies use when considering the use of telecommunications lines: faster and smaller equals better. The faster a signal can move over a line, the less cost there will be for using the line (even though faster lines usually cost a little more). Speed is also important because users don't want to wait for large files such as pictures, sound or video to arrive. For example, no one wants to sit at their computer and wait two minutes while a digital photograph (potentially a very large file size) slowly appears on the screen.

By increasing compression, more information can be delivered in a shorter period of time. To further illustrate the need for compression, consider this: without compression, one full frame of digital television requires almost 1 megabyte of storage. Uncompressed, a 10-second clip of digital television would consume a 300 megabyte hard drive (at standard 30 frames per second). However, it must be kept in mind that there is a significant difference between 'real-time' video transmitted in a video teleconference, and video which is stored on a hard disk. In a live teleconference, users can't (and won't) wait for chuncks of video to appear...it must be real-time. Uncompressed, real-time video requires the transmission of 90 million bits per second!

Table 6-2 illustrates how compression technology has dramatically enhanced the ability to send video signals over smaller and smaller bandwidth, while transmission costs simultaneously continue to drop.

Coaxial cable represent another route on the information highway. Tele-Communications Inc. (TCI), the nation's largest cable company, operates the $100 million National Digital Television Center in Colorado. The facility uses digital compression

Table 6-2   Transmission Rates for Compressed Video and the Cost of Leasing Circuits

Year	Transmission Rate for Compressed Video	Approximate Cost for Transcontinental Public Switched Networks, 56 Circuits
1994	768 Kbps	$200/hour
1994	224 Kbps	$150/hour
1994	128 Kbps	$25/hour
1994	56 Kbps	$15/hour

technology to send as many as ten television channel signals in the space normally filled by one signal. The result? The capacity to deliver 500 television channels, provide interactive services, transmit computer data and information, and offer videoconferencing and video-on-demand to homes and businesses.

A second challenge has been the lack of compatibility between different manufacturers' equipment, and the different technologies that allow video and multimedia signals to be processed on the PC. In 1990 the CCITT (now ITU-TSS) established H.320, a set of videoconferencing standards that promote interoperability between manufacturers. This standard may also signal a transition from proprietary technology, as noted in an article in *Data Communications*:

> "Makers of videoconferencing equipment expect systems based on standard-issue PCs to outsell products based on proprietary hardware by a two-to-one margin this year—a remarkable development given the fact that the first PC-based desk-top offerings debuted only two years ago, while conventional videoconferencing systems have been available since the early 1980s."[3]

3. Elliot M. Gold, "PCs Rewrite the Rules for Videoconferencing," *Data Communications*, March 1994, p. 95.

Perhaps the most significant challenge is the cost required to implement video and multimedia technology. When organizations have an installed base of thousands of personal computers, the economic impact of upgrading PCs for video is enormous.

Technology Spawns Practical Applications

Now that the technology offers real-time interactive transmission of video and computer information, applications are blooming. Companies conduct multipoint training presentations where a speaker talks to hundreds, even thousands, of employees at several locations simultaneously. Business meetings occur between individuals at locations around the world. Health care professionals use the technology to transmit patient information and medical lab reports during on-line, interactive discussions. Figure 6-2 shows a videoconferencing room, and Figure 6-3 illustrates videoconferencing implementation.

U S WEST Communications, one of the regional bell operating companies (RBOCs), provides communications services and data solutions to more than 25 million residential and business customers in 14 western and midwestern states. Referring to this company as a "Baby Bell" would be more than an understatement. With revenues that exceed $10 billion, U S WEST is a global communications firm with business activities that include communications, information, marketing and financial services. It has subsidiaries in directory publishing, cellular communications and paging, international cable television and financial services.

In its endeavors, U S WEST continues to blur the boundaries between information, entertainment, computer data and communications as it develops strategic alliances with major

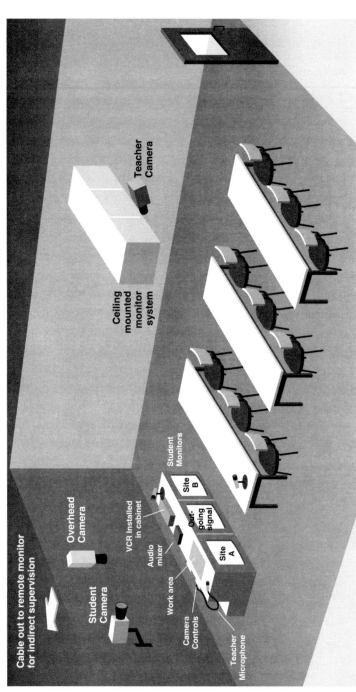

Figure 6–2 Typical setup for a video conferencing room. (Courtesy U S West)

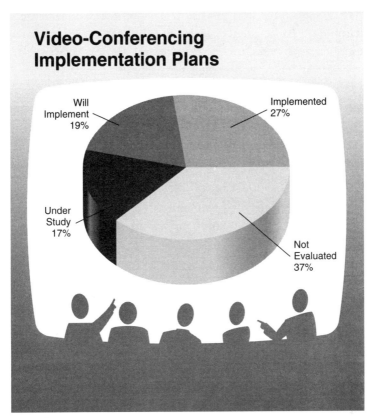

Video-Conferencing Implementation Plans

Will Implement 19%

Implemented 27%

Under Study 17%

Not Evaluated 37%

Figure 6–3

players that include Tele-Communications, Inc. (the world's largest cable TV system operation) and Time Warner (the world's largest media and entertainment company). U S WEST International develops, builds and operates telecommunications systems in Europe and other attractive markets.

One of the subsidiaries of U S WEST is Business and Government Services. This subsidiary helps businesses, schools and government operations with both the connection and application of video, voice and data communications. Dr.

Greg Voeltz, an account executive, specializes in the use of technology for distance learning applications. Dr. Voeltz describes one version of this technology which, with a large-screen setup, is designed for use with groups of 2 to 20 individuals. "While using this system to transmit video and voice, users also have the ability to fully interact with personal computers," he notes. "Users share data and files from computer to computer, making changes on-line, and completing complex transactions. This is an integrated unit. Users move effortlessly from video to computer information."

The technology is best suited for situations in which information or courses could or would not be offered. U S WEST covers 14 rural states, each of which may have two or three large metropolitan areas. "Historically, we would fly employees from Wyoming, Montana or Idaho into a major metropolitan area like Denver or Minneapolis," notes Dr. Voeltz. "Today we conduct this training on-line, using the network. We have found that as long as it is fully interactive, this technology works extremely well. It reduces travel expenses significantly, expands the number of employees we can train and broadens opportunities for the presentation of different types of knowledge. There are no limitations—you can offer this service virtually anyplace there is a telephone line."

Douglas Brush of D/J Brush Associates believes cost savings realized from reduction in travel is only one of the benefits of videoconferencing. He says, "The reason video has been so popular over the years is that it is the second best replacement for face-to-face communications. Unfortunately, video is not interactive in the linear tape format. Videoconferencing is coming on very strong for that reason. Clients have told us it is popular because it offsets travel costs. That is a secondary benefit. The primary benefit is the on-line, dynamic management of communications. It increases productivity and improves the decision-making process. And it allows more people in different departments who may be involved in a project to become directly involved in the communication."

IBM has a television network that links sites in the U.S and Canada, reaching approximately 90% of its U.S. workforce. The company has daily news broadcasts, with usually three or four stories about new products, customer solutions, directional statements and community support stories. IBM's Andy McCormick discusses videoconferencing: "We have more than 100 sites around the world where you can have video conferences. About 35 of the sites in the U.S. have full-motion videoconferencing. Finance, marketing, accounting, product development—all departments use those."

Putting Video onto the PC

Bruce McKenzie, President of Business Information Graphics, points out that sending video and graphics to workstations increases the power of the message. He says, "Assuming you have something that you need to communicate to your employees, you can communicate it in a way that is more involving. You have a better chance of getting your message across by using a powerful communication medium with motion and color, which is what humans respond to. "

In addition to being more powerful, communications that use visuals and sound are more likely to be understood and remembered. Microsoft's Mark Protus explains: "Studies show that approximately 50% of people learn visually, about 30% learn auditorially and about 20% learn through textual information. I don't know if that is shifting, but having video, audio and text allows you to cover a lot of different ways that people learn. Often, you can learn without having text by watching how somebody else does it. Many computer products are just chock full of information. Now you've got different ways to access and use that information." Figure 6-4 shows the ability of multimedia to help people learn.

Figure 6–4   Multimedia accommodates the fact that different people use different senses for learning.

Protus believes that local area networks are a good distribution vehicle for multimedia. LAN-based communications, he emphasizes, provide a storage media that is capable of holding a variety of different information. This technology allows people over long distances to access quality video or audio. Running multimedia on a network opens up the potential for interactive communications where several people can be online at the same time.

Brian White of GTE agrees, explaining that as costs decline, the appeal of sending video directly to the workstations increases. He says, "There is a very good opportunity that as the communications infrastructure grows in the United States, the cost of delivering more complex data over the telephone line will become less expensive. It only makes sense for GTE to position for that now. One driver is the multisensory appeal of the information. As the communications marketplace becomes more cluttered, we constantly look for something to give our message an edge that will help get that message across."

American Express has also moved toward pushing video to employees' desktop computers. The company is building a system that allows about 7,000 employees at corporate headquarters in New York to access video on their computers. Recognizing that world events shape markets and opportunities, employees can receive live broadcasts from sources like CNN.

"Essentially, it is desktop multimedia, delivering video and a whole menu of information options to employees over their PC screens," describes Ron Martin, former Vice President of Corporate Employee Communications. "Video communications played an important role during the Persian Gulf War. During the early part of the war we kept CNN up live, full-time, on our video monitors. Not only did people have a desire to stay abreast of what was happening, but world events influence the financial markets. People keep their ears open to what's happening outside the company. So with this capability, we ensure that people can access external news sources as well as receive information from within the company."

Martin explains that video has an impact in part because it provides information in a medium and a format to which employees are accustomed. American Express emulates the six o'clock news, using an anchor person and short news reports. By recreating the look of a television newscast, employees are made receptive to the information.

However, unlike IBM or Federal Express, American Express has pursued distribution of video on the PC network. Martin says, "We didn't go the satellite transmission route like Federal Express because I believe that over the long term, delivery to desktops—systems-based delivery—is going to be more efficient and less costly. American Express already had much of the infrastructure in place. And many employees work in a situation where they can receive video at their workstations."

Martin believes that video on the desktop may be produced in even shorter segments than those people currently see on television. He says, "Every medium has limitations, and any video that runs more than six or seven minutes is going to lose people. Once you start putting it on a menu and delivering it to PC screens, you're probably talking about breaking it up into 30-second segments. We need to experiment with this to determine the best length. We will always need print to cover issues in depth. Print will always supplement electronic media and visa versa because they do different things."

Douglas Brush agrees that desktop video is unique. Producers, he says, create desktop images (still-frame or compressed) faster and for less money than traditional video. Also, users receive desktop images faster over a PC network than through traditional delivery systems. This creates new opportunities to use video where it could not have been used previously. Brush cites one example: "One corporation outside Boston has a wonderful down-and-dirty system. It is a stand-alone, PC-based system that can hook into the mainframe to create at desktop locations what we call 'disposable video.' It is economical enough to do a video training program for one individual for one-time use, or it can be transmitted to all locations throughout the network. If it changes, you simply transmit the changes."

The results of a nationwide survey by Douglas and Judith Brush indicate that video communications professionals are actively developing systems that deliver video to the workstation. They write:

"While only 68% of the video respondents are using general purpose computers in their operations, 86% said that they are involved in the planning of office automation in their organizations, particularly in the use of "Local Area Networks" (LANs)...We asked the study respondents to give us their opinion about the desirability of a LAN system which would permit the delivery of full-motion color video along with data and other forms of communications to every terminal or workstation in their operation. Only 11% of those answering said that such an installation was not desirable. The remaining 89% were more visionary. One-quarter said the installation would be highly desirable, more than likely envisioning the various types of communications needs they would fulfill with it. Another 22% said it would be somewhat desirable, while 42% said it would possibly be desirable." [4]

---

4. Douglas and Judith Brush, *Private Television Communications: New Directions—The Fourth Brush Report.*

Merrill Lynch is distributing video to desktop computers. Ritch Gaiti, First Vice-President of Advanced Office Systems, explains: "We're just experimenting with it now. First, pictures talk far more than words do, and they communicate better for certain things. We look for breaking news-items that need attention. Video is very effective. We have our own internal direct-broadcast satellite system, a closed-circuit system that we use to educate our financial consultants, to announce new products and discuss new strategies."

"We are experimenting to integrate the closed-circuit system into the workstation so it can be used for training, announcements and breaking news. We have video working on an experimental basis on about 65 workstations throughout the country. The concept is to bring information, in a form that people might be able to use better, right up to the workstation."

The system at Merrill Lynch lets employees' choose a video option on their PC. Programming can be accessed any time. There are three choices today. One is internal broadcasts. A second is an internal in-the-office videotape, and the third is CNBC/FNN. Users simply select the channel of their choice.

A Videoconference in Your Office

A logical extension of distributing video to employees computers is conducting videoconferences via computer. By using computers that have video cameras and microphones, images, sound and graphics can be transmitted between participants. To process video, graphics and sound effectively, users require a multimedia PC (MPC). Typically, this is a 386 or 486 PC that has at least 8 megabytes of random access memory (RAM), a video board that supports NTSC (National Television Standards Committee) motion video, video and audio codecs (coder/decoder) and a video camera, scanner and audio microphones. It also requires software that supports these applications. Figure 6-5 shows PC videoconferencing.

Figure 6–5 Transmitting full-color, full-motion video and graphics directly to their desktop PCs, sales managers in Boston and London can work collaboratively on a proposal for a multinational account using the Picture-Tel LIVE PCS 100. (Photo courtesy PictureTel)

An MPC connected to a LAN offers tremendous opportunities to increase the effectiveness of meetings. Interactive video communication creates new applications when participants can exchange electronic information, data and files from computers simultaneously with the video. Users can share data that is available on the computer network. In an article in Video Systems magazine, Basil Halhed and D. Lynn Scott discuss this advantage:

"When the MPC (multimedia PC) is connected to a LAN and server, the server's hard disk can store still images, data and programs, making them accessible from any connected PC or workstation before or after a multimedia conference. This means that whatever support materials you need for your conference can be prepared on your PC. Rather than generate printouts and graphics beforehand, you can just access data as needed from the server during the conference."[5]

U S WEST has applications where employees connect visually via PC. "It is a form of interactive television using desktop PCs," explains Dr. Voeltz. "However, this system uses slower transmission speeds, potentially as slow as 56 Kb. In this environment we find that the video remains acceptable, and the audio quality is outstanding. You have a personal screen (a 5" screen) literally mounted on top of the PC. U S WEST uses this technology today. For example, we connect between our Denver office and our research center in Boulder, Colorado. I could go to a computer and see the person I am speaking with on this screen."

Video is an important communications tool at Hewlett-Packard. In addition to HP's video broadcast and videoconferencing capabilities, the company is experimenting with the delivery of "on-demand" video directly to PCs and workstations via the LAN. Randall Whiting, Manager of Worldwide Electronic Sales Promotion, believes this technology will allow the company to fully integrate video into personal communications. He says, "These capabilities will enable personal vid-

5. Basil Halhed and D. Lynn Scott, "Making Multimedia Conferencing Work for You," Supplement to *Video Systems*, December 1991, p. 3.

eoconferencing or allow access to archives of digital videos of presentations and meetings."

Tom Martin at Federal Express believes that the challenges associated with pushing interactive video onto PCs make it unlikely that all offices will have it in the near future. He says, "One limitation is that you have to retrofit computers to accept either coaxial cable or digitized video. Digitized video is really not quite there yet when you compare the quality to full-motion analog signals. Those signals can only be carried over coaxial cable. Of course, there are some computers today that could accept coaxial cable input, and you can feed video into the system. That usually requires some modification to put it on the screen along with data. As with most companies, we've got all types of computer terminals. To configure all of these to accept video requires a huge capital expenditure."

Martin Nisenholtz of Ogilvy & Mather Direct agrees that costs must come down, and believes that in the near future networks as well as personal computers will be configured to accept video. "In 1994 you have video on the computer motherboard, so every computer sold will be able to play video. Once you've got that, you need to have local area networks that can deal with video efficiently. There are certain costs in the networks themselves. Compression technologies that exist today can handle that for small LANs."

The growth in the delivery and application of PC-based video is sure to continue. Video compression technology continues to improve; add-on video boards allow PCs to display full-screen broadcast-quality video and specialty servers, which provide on-demand digital video across the market, are now available. The industry research firm Dataquest, Incorporated predicts that the market for video servers will grow exponentially, exceeding $5 billion dollars in revenues by 1997. See Figure 6-6.

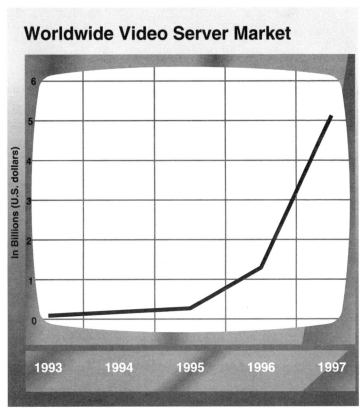

Figure 6–6 Worldwide video server market growth. (Courtesy Dataquest.)

Hypertext to the Rescue

One downside to delivering a tremendous amount of information to employees via their computers is that the end result can be confusion. Advanced communications software now helps users find what they are looking for.

"Hypertext" is the term that describes computer-delivered documentation where viewers move through information in a nonlinear fashion. Nonlinear refers to the fact that users don't access information in the traditional beginning-to-end fashion. With a book, for example, readers normally start at page one and then read to the end, page by page. With nonlinear computer documents readers move randomly, through a series of computer links, to different parts of a document. Nonlinear reading allows the reader (not the document) to decide what information is important.

NTERGAID has been developing, selling and promoting hypertext software for more than five years. Company President Scott Johnson believes hypertext is catching on because it helps readers get what they want faster. He says, "Communicators realize cost and efficiency benefits, but hypertext is really a reader's paradise. Accessing factual information is not really reading, it is retrieving. It involves looking for things that interest us. Then we read. With hypertext, readers have some significant capabilities. They can map documents, they can search, and they have several ways to get through the information. Each person retrieves a little differently because their jobs are all different. Hypertext is simply a better retrieval system."

Organizations benefit when employees/readers can find information rapidly. Integrating text and graphics right to the computer guarantees that information is current. As a result, employees don't look up incorrect or out-of-date information, which they then act upon. Says Johnson, "How often have we seen mistakes in the corporate purchasing world where someone bought the wrong thing, or did it the wrong way? The company pays for it. You can't hold anybody accountable for it if they simply have the wrong version of the paper. Another benefit is cost savings. The amount of paper we all create is absurd. If you create it on computer, you can distribute it on computer. A further benefit is ease of access. You make the assumption that employees are ethical people who will do the right thing if it is not too hard. If I have to go look up something in a big manual, or search my desk for a newsletter, it is tough. However, if I can sit at my desk, point and click, it will get checked and it will get done."

NTERGAID HyperWriter! software creates applications ranging from stand-alone training to LAN-based corporate communications. Johnson provides one application example. "Metal Castings Technologies is a subsidiary of General Motors. They develop engine heads. Here is a very technical company. They've got a complex body of information about engine heads. They use HyperWriter! as a way to convey information from Metal Casting Technology engineers back to GM Corporate. So they use it to distribute research information and highly technical material with pictures. Now, if I'm an engineer from General Motors and I get that HyperWriter! material, I can annotate it, look at it, put graphic files into a report for my boss, or take the text out for analysis in a database program or spreadsheet. When you start moving on-line it becomes very powerful. Data analysis often fails simply because the information is not all electronic. If we go all-electronic, we let readers draw their own conclusions. The more involved we can make workers, the more they can do for us."

Multimedia: It's All Things to All People

The integration of text, visuals and audio creates many new applications for communicators. Members of the International Interactive Communications Society (IICS) often develop these applications. With more than 4,500 members around the world, the IICS is an international nonprofit professional organization that promotes the use of interactive communications. Deborah Palm, IICS Managing Director, describes how one member applies interactive communications to archive and access visual information. "This application uses a Macintosh computer with HyperCard, a laserdisk player and a monitor. The objective is to replace large slide and microfiche collections with a durable, modifiable and space-efficient storage and retrieval system."

Tony Van Atta, Program Manager of Documentation Information Services at Northern Telecom, believes that merging text, video and audio improves the effectiveness of documentation. "My favorite example," he says enthusiastically, "is that I'm looking at an automobile repair manual, and I come to a section on removing a carburetor. It says, "Do you know how to remove the carburetor?" If you say no, you see a little icon that looks like a motion picture camera. You click on that, and it pops up a little window where you can see somebody taking off a carburetor. You continue through the manual, and it says, 'Adjust the carburetor until it sounds smooth.' You don't know what smooth sounds like, so you click on another button to hear what it should sound like. This is where documents are going today."

Van Atta does have concerns. Regarding standards, he says, "The real issue from my standpoint is that I don't have a universal standard. I can already do that on the Macintosh, but I can't do it with the box that is available in the MS-DOS world. If users buy a $500 board and plug into the MS-DOS box, they can do it. But it means separate animation and sound for PC, Macintosh and UNIX. Quality is another issue. It is not network-TV-quality. People see high-quality production at home. They are not going to accept anything less."

Nevertheless, multimedia is proliferating. It represents big business as hardware manufacturers move toward standards, and software companies improve the capabilities and user-friendly nature of multimedia programs. A Business Research Group survey indicates that between 1990 and 1995, the use of desktop multimedia will increase significantly (see Figure 6-7).

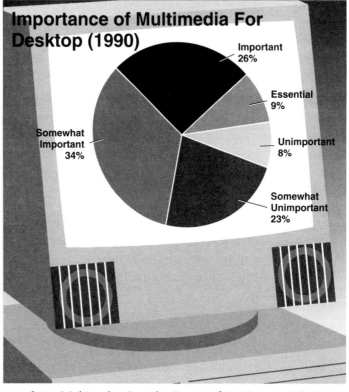

Figure 6–7 Multimedia Growth (Part 1 of 2) (Courtesy The Business Research Group.)

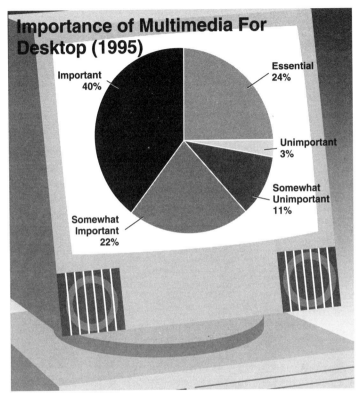

Essential 24%

Important 40%

Unimportant 3%

Somewhat Unimportant 11%

Somewhat Important 22%

Importance of Multimedia For Desktop (1995)

Figure 6–7 Multimedia Growth (Part 2 of 2) (Courtesy The Business Research Group.)

Located outside of Boston, Wonder Corp. provides clients with products and applications ranging from multimedia electronic mail to interactive desktop training. Paras Traganos, President of Wonder Corp., argues that organizations do not have to wait for future developments or spend excessive sums of money to use multimedia today. He says, "When we talk about multimedia, we say available now because companies currently have the platforms in place to do it. Applications that proliferate today take advantage of the existing infrastructure."

Several Wonder Corp. clients use multimedia for internal communications. They keep costs down and maintain system flexibility by distributing information on computer disk. "In terms of corporate communications, multimedia is going to change the way we communicate to the field. It will make it more personal by getting away from paper and allowing people to be entertained," explains Traganos.

One Wonder Corp. customer, Landmark Graphics, has service engineers in 26 countries. Landmark Graphics produces high-end workstations, costing up to $500,000. These computers perform seismic interpretation for the oil, gas and mineral exploration marketplaces. Landmark sent an interactive disk to employees. The first image that appears is corporate headquarters in Houston. A voice says, "Press 1, 2, 3 or 4." Press 1. The CEO appears on screen and says, "I want to tell you that if these systems weren't maintained properly, we wouldn't be growing as fast as we have been." Press 2: "Hi, I'm the CFO, and I want to tell you that the service division is the most profitable." Another customer, Marshall's, uses Wonder Corp. equipment in 400 department stores. They produce and distribute a weekly news briefing from corporate headquarters.

Press F1 When You Need an Expert: Problem-Solving and Training Applications

Computers become more useful when they work with users to solve problems. Expert systems represent a branch of artificial intelligence in which computers help users analyze and solve complex problems. To accomplish this, an expert system captures the knowledge and problem-solving skills of human experts and develops them into a computer program. As a result, nontechnical people can take advantage of the skills of an expert. By asking a series of questions and retrieving information from other computer databases, the computer guides users through a problem and develops a competent solution or produces needed information.

In their book *The Rise of the Expert Company*, Edward Feigenbaum, Pamela McCorduck and H. Penny Nii suggest that computer-based libraries should do more than simply help users find information. The authors write:

> "The libraries of today are warehouses for passive objects. The books and journals sit on shelves, waiting for us to use our intelligence to find them, read them, interpret them and finally make them divulge their stored knowledge. 'Electronic' libraries of today are no better. Their pages are pages of data files, but the electronic page images are equally passive... Now imagine the library as an active, intelligent 'knowledge server.' It stores knowledge in complete knowledge structures (perhaps in a formalism yet to be invented) so that crossovers and connections between categories are routine. It can use its knowledge to assist its users in problem solving and other complex thinking tasks."[6]

Jay Gondelman is the owner of Interactive Engineering, a Chicago-based firm that specializes in the development of multimedia for advertising applications. According to Gondelman, the medium is most effective when it helps people locate information and accomplish tasks. "There are two significant applications for interactive computing and multimedia," stresses Gondelman. "One is when a user can go directly to the information they need, jumping from area to area in a rapid, nonlinear fashion. The second is when a user provides information

---

6. Edward Feigenbaum, Pamela McCorduck, and H. Penny Nii, *The Rise of the Expert Company*, Times Books, p. 256.

about a problem, and the program then works with this information and provides an answer. This goes far beyond simply reading text. Users must think about what they input. The computer, meanwhile, walks them through tasks which may involve complex calculations, and performs the evaluation."

Cathy Flowers of SRI International also believes problem-solving is a key application for computer-based communications. She explains: "We are working with multimedia, which is going to be a very strong promotional device in the next few years. Customers can get a sophisticated information package very quickly. For example, we worked with the investment promotion organization of the Dominican Republic to develop a multimedia sales package. A potential client can sit at a keyboard and access a variety of types of information ranging from free trade zone rules to tax structures. That system was very flexible and could provide highly focused information to meet a specific client's needs."

American manufacturers plunk down approximately $45 billion dollars annually in the pursuit of employee training and education.[7] Training is a natural for multimedia, especially when information is delivered directly to an individual PC from the network. One of the reasons to put training programs on a network is that it enhances and accelerates the ability to change and update the information/training. It facilitates both change and the specialization of training. The endusers receive the training they require when they need it— just-in-time training.

"We do an enormous amount of training both in the United States and around the world," notes Arthur Andersen's Eric Dean. "Historically, the delivery vehicle has occurred in

---

7. October 1992 Industry Report, *Training Magazine.*

classroom time. Over the past decade we have been doing more and more computer based training (CBT). Today, this is delivered on videodiscs and CD-ROMs. The natural evolution is to place this onto the network, enabling people to select training out of the same network over which they receive other reference material.

"You might have a core program that encompasses the basics. You add branches to enhance and specialize the training. This works extremely well when the training doesn't have to be delivered in a classroom, where there is a finite period of training time. Rather, this is a path that an individual can follow. A broad web of material becomes available to them. Having it on a network is the training equivalent of 'video on demand.'"

Communicators must familiarize themselves with the hardware and software tools that produce and distribute multimedia documents. Payoffs are significant because communication that integrates text, video, graphics and sound is significantly more effective than communication that does not. Delivery of multimedia messages directly to employees' personal computers increases the power of the communications. Hypertext document retrieval software and computer expert systems boost productivity further as they help employees find information and solve complex problems.

Making It Work:
Implementation and Training

Collection, preservation and retrieval of information in a timely and useful form for the end user is a major goal if we are to build and maintain a productive, competitive work force in an interconnected global market.

—Summary Report, White House Conference on Library and Information Services

Organizations realize tremendous payoffs from delivering information and data to employees directly on their desktop computers. Rarely, however, is communication the motivating force when organizations develop and install a computer infrastructure. Applications such as access to mainframe databases, or use of word processor or spreadsheet software, initially motivate the installation of LANs and WANs.

This chapter focuses on procedures that help communication professionals successfully develop applications that utilize existing or planned computer infrastructures. Communicators need to maintain responsibility for designing their applications, and they must insist that the information services department help develop a system that fulfills their needs.

Analyzing the Needs of the Organization

Sarah Norton, Director of Marketing for Massachusetts-based Business Research Group, knows that successful implementation requires planning. She says, "Companies that preplan the use of technology see a return on their investment. Companies that do not develop a strategy or make allowances for training employees don't realize the productivity gains they expect."

Organizations must undergo a detailed process to determine the value of the technology. This process involves a group-by-group assessment of communication flow. It begins with a needs analysis which examines the work that people have, their responsibilities, mandates and work habits. The data from this analysis determines who needs what, and why. It also identifies the type and extent of training that will be required.

Organizations benefit from hiring consultants to assist with a technology and applications analysis. Bernard Mathaisel of Ernst & Young explains, "We are a consulting service. I will visit a firm tomorrow that wants a global record management system. It is an expensive, large undertaking. They have to decide first what information will serve current and prospective needs. Next, they need to decide what technology to platform this on. They need to decide what mode to store documents in, and they need to arrive at a policy to determine what documents to store. These are the type of issues that firms can use consultants for."

He adds, "We advise on information technology infrastructures or architecture. We help clients arrive at enterprise-wide standards for linking and structuring their information systems. We go beyond networking standards to look at what type of standards they want to institute for workstations. Should they allow each division to go off and do their own thing, or should there be corporate standards? It really depends upon the specifics of the business need, the best of available technology and the corporate culture."

Following are some questions that must be addressed when developing a new communications application that will use a computer network for distribution.

Needs Analysis

The System

1. How many employees are/will be connected?

2. How many sites will be connected?

3. How many employees/viewers will be simultaneously viewing information?

4. To what extent is the organization already connected electronically?

5. What computers do employees use (quantity and types)?

6. Are there standards in place (hardware and software)?

7. What are the speeds of telecommunications lines to different sites?

8. What response time is required/acceptable for retrieval of documents?

The Application

1. What is the application (current and future)?

2. How many employees will benefit from the application?

3. How often will this communication be used?

4. If electronic communications will be replacing an existing form of communication (i.e., a publication), what are the current costs of production and distribution?

Documents

1. What is the nature of the electronic documents?
   - Communications
   - Customer information / orders
   - Financial
   - Policies, procedures, organizational directories

2. What are the characteristics of the documents:
   - Is color required?
   - Will graphics, pictures, drawings or charts be used?
   - How many pages are the documents?

3. What administration is required with the documents:
   - How frequently will documents be written or updated?
   - Will old documents be deleted or stay for archival reference?
   - Will/must documents be date-stamped?

- Will existing hard-copy documentation be converted to electronic form?
- How many new pages will be added to the documents on a weekly or monthly basis?

Special Feature Requirements

1. What types of information searching is required by viewers?
   - Index
   - Word
   - Boolean
   - Phonetic

2. Do documents require hypertext links for navigation?

3. What security is required?
   - By authors
   - By viewers

4. Does the system offer on-line help or tutorials?

5. Should viewers be able to print out the documents on local printers?

6. Do viewers need an alert for notification of new documents being added?

7. For navigation, do viewers require any type of 'history' or path function?

Implementation

1. What department has the application (i.e., who is the application owner)?

2. What departments need to get involved to implement the application?

3. How long will it take to get the system on-line?

4. What are the training ramifications?

Communications Flow Analysis

1. How does this information get distributed currently?

2. Who sees the information?

3. Does the information require feedback from the target audience? Will it be a two-way system?

Cost Considerations

1. Hardware
   - System
   - End-user

2. Software and programming
   - Purchase
   - Develop in-house

3. Training

4. Application support

How Quickly Can Things Change Around Here?

New communication technology appears on the marketplace daily. This makes it difficult for organizations, information systems and communications professionals to test and review the technology and make purchasing decisions. In addition, the cost of hardware and software prohibits buying new equipment frequently.

Bud Mathaisel believes that the life cycle of technology depends upon to whom you talk. He has developed a timetable he calls the 18, 36, 60 framework, referring to the number of months in a life cycle for changeovers to occur. The framework can be visualized as three concentric circles, each dependent on the next inner circle. The inner circle represents technology vendors, who achieve technological breakthroughs and would like to replace basic technology like circuits every 18 months. Software vendors are the next outer circle. It takes these vendors approximately three years to fully develop new software for the new technologies. The outside circle, the endusers, are at 60 months. Mathaisel notes that even in progressive companies, CEOs are unwilling to throw away their infrastructure investment more frequently than every five years. Thus, the rate of change-over on applications is about 60 months.

"I had a very aggressive approach to depreciation of technologies as Chief Information Officer (at Disney) and advertised it as such," says Mathaisel. "Independent of what the tax rules were, our thought process for justifying new technologies was to depreciate everything three years to zero, knowing that some technologies may pull out in two years, others maybe four. Software that was infrastructure software, we would justify on a depreciation life of five years to zero…payroll, general ledger, whatever else. That is more rapid than normal tax rules, as well as the mentality and investment realities of large corporations. We are talking about a company having 8,000 PCs and having the potential for throwing them out every three years."

For many organizations, the decision to move ahead with communications technology is based more on the need to remain competitive than on the exact return on investment from the technology. That has been the case with MasterCard. "Our biggest challenge was convincing people that e-mail can make a difference," recalls Karyn Mardis. "What helped was that MasterCard had five goals, and one of those was to become a truly global company. Our logic has been that we cannot do that without electronic communications, so decisions were based on strategic advantage."

Having good applications and realizing bottom-line benefits are not the only considerations. Employees must be willing to embrace and use technology, or it will not succeed. Employee acceptance depends upon several factors. First, new technologies must be phased in carefully. Otherwise, employees feel overwhelmed. Second, a training and end-user support system must be developed.

Sarah Norton says, "It is more a human issue than a numbers issue. We went through a great transition in technology, and it is an evolving process. People had just gotten used to their individual workstations when capabilities such as electronic mail and multimedia came along. Often the work force is not ready for what is available technically. We see that in the 90s with the slowdown of the purchase of bells and whistles. Particularly in America, we tend to be quick to jump on new technologies. Now we are in an era where we have enough technology. We need to understand what we're doing with all of this."

Martin Nisenholtz, Senior Vice President at Ogilvy and Mather Direct, concurs. "The main stumbling block is that there is a certain inertia in any business," he says. "It is not easy to change the way people do things even if you can show that the new way is better. Number one, people have to know why new technology is installed. This is a problem. Often technologies are put in place by MIS people. Business is going along fine from the users' point of view. They have no reason to change because they're not in the business of exploring technology. However, if you don't get this technology out into the real world, it remains theoretical."

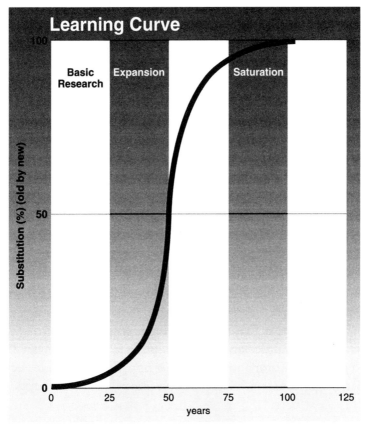

Figure 7–1   Historically, there is about a 50-year period of time between the initial introduction of a new technology and the time at which that technology saturates the marketplace.

Historically, it takes approximately 50 to 75 years for new technology to move from invention to complete utilization in the marketplace. Nisenholtz believes that the curve on this timeline will become steeper with advanced communications technologies. He says, "These curves accelerate in certain circumstances. It took 50 years for the telephone to achieve 50% penetration. Part of the explanation for that was that in the late 19th century, there were few reasons for people to talk on the telephone. There may be more reasons for people to share information. It won't necessarily require 50 years to achieve 50% penetration of this technology in a company…a period of 50 years represents a long time in the late 20th century." Figure 7-1 shows the timeline for technology market saturation.

Who Makes the Decision?

It can be difficult to decide which departments in an organization make the decision to create and implement computer-based communication applications. The information services department has an interest in the development and maintenance of the system from a technological point of view. Most organizations also depend upon information services to perform training and support functions.

A battle that frequently develops centers around the fact that it is the endusers, not information services personnel, who have specific information needs. Endusers also have an interest in the development of their applications. It is the business unit, the department, the enduser who has a specific communications need. The requirement may be to electronically distribute employee benefit enrollment procedures and forms, or to tie into a financial information database, automatically cull the stock prices of competitors and send this information out to site managers. In almost every instance the application, not the technology, should drive the development of an appropriate solution.

Bernard Mathaisel of Ernst & Young addresses the issue. He says, "The coinage of the phrase 'technology services manager' comes from the notion that 'chief information officer' was a misnomer. The information is the property, the responsibility and the asset of individual knowledge workers. The IS organization's job is to provide the infrastructure to allow that to happen, then to get out of the way."

Douglas Brush of D/J Brush Associates believes that end-user needs are especially important in the realm of multimedia and video. He says, "Video has always been a user-driven activity. Data communication is generally a technology driven by data systems people and telecommunications people. They impose technology on users who don't quite know what to do with it. If we let users determine the technology, there would be better progress."

One area where compromise may be beneficial is standardization. In decentralized organizations the lack of computer standardization, in both hardware and software, hinders communications. New computer communication applications should be developed with an understanding of the existing (and future) computer infrastructure. This approach ensures that a terrific application that may initially have a limited audience, such as an executive information system, can easily be expanded to broader audiences.

Communication applications are easy to implement because they use existing system architecture and hardware. These technologies can absolutely be cost-justified, exclaims Paras Traganos, President of Wonder Corp. According to Traganos, the real key is to take advantage of the installed base of workstations by using software to integrate applications on existing platforms, using existing networks. Traganos believes that it is necessary to pilot an application to ensure reasonable cost justification and successful implementation. He says, "For any company to run an enterprise-wide solution, you really have to pilot it first. If you go to an electronic mail function, the problem arises that when you do the pilot, only a subset of employees use it. And if you only communicate with a subset, the costs exceed the savings. What organizations need to do is focus on finite work group applications where managers can calculate dollars saved."

"The data processing or information services department will pay for it, or a corporate officer who is going to use it in a particular application...sales training, field service training, marketing, merchandising. To bring multimedia into a large corporation in a big fashion, you have to have somebody bring you in on a small pilot. They need an immediate gut reaction that says, 'I know this is going to save me money.' At that point, your internal champion garners support from other parts of the corporation. The real key is to get the successful pilot in there where someone can figure out the cost justification. Because in the end, all these people report to shareholders."

Is Big Better?

Small organizations implement technology faster than large ones. There are several reasons for this. Small organizations do not have large bureaucracies that slow down the process of approval and implementation. Smaller firms react faster because they don't have any preconceived ideas about how things should be done. Widespread implementation of the technology occurs quickly in a small company as 100% of the employees rapidly receive the technology. Also, small organizations do not require long-term commitment to the technology, and they are not mainframe-oriented.

Although large organizations may not be able to implement the technology as quickly as small firms, the payback may be far greater for them. When thousands of employees are able to receive communications instantaneously, work at home or eliminate paper production, cost savings quickly add up. NTERGAID's Scott Johnson acknowledges pros and cons to organizational size. "Large companies see bigger payback," he says. "If you've got 10,000 workers, you're going to see more significant payback than if the company has 100 or 200 workers. A small company usually can't devote the resources to a project to do it right, the way a big company can. However, in a smaller company people adapt to the technology faster, adopt it and use it."

Centralized Versus Decentralized

Beyond organizational size, implementation is affected by an organization's decision to create either a centralized or decentralized system. Technically, a centralized system uses one central file server or mainframe, which is accessed by employees at sites across the country. The advantage to this type of system architecture is that it is easier from an administrative point of view. All of the electronic documents are in one location. This eliminates concern over which version of a document employees are looking at.

A decentralized system allows regional hubs or local sites to download information from a central file server or mainframe and then redistribute this information. The advantage to a decentralized structure is that regional or local sites can add documents that are of interest to employees in that region or site to the document database. Technically, by downloading and redistributing documents, readers are able to access documents faster. The disadvantage is that a decentralized structure

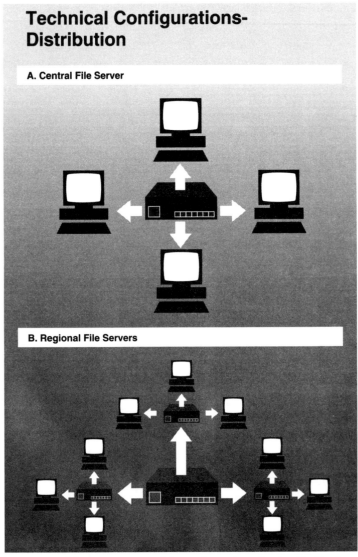

Figure 7–2 There are two possible configurations for the distribution of electronic documents. A centralized file server stores all documents in one location, whereas a decentralized system sends the documents out to reside in regional file servers.

requires more administrative work (from an information systems point of view) at the local level. Also, depending when documents are downloaded, the information will not be as current as in a centralized system. Figure 7-2 illustrates the centralized and decentralized distribution configurations.

Ritch Gaiti, First Vice-President of Advanced Office Systems at Merrill Lynch, talks about the issues. He says, "The speed of these technologies enables companies to move data a lot faster than before. As a result, you can localize a significant amount of processing. Each organization has to look at how that can be applied within their own business. By having more local processing, you cut down on errors and make departments more self-sufficient."

Scott Johnson lists some of the pros and cons of a centralized system: "The pro is that it is easy to maintain. Everybody gets information from a uniform source. Largely, that is a technical pro. The cons are that you've got higher costs of access and decreased access speed. If you've got decreased access speed, people are less likely to use it. At some point the cost of dialing in gets prohibitive. What can you do about that? Well, you could look into replication facilities whereby you replicate the database at other sites across the country and then access out from those sites. The big question is the size of data involved. To save time, you can replicate only files that have changed."

Don't Forget Training

The single most important, yet often overlooked, aspect of implementation is training. There are two groups of people that need to be trained. One group is the employees who will be developing and using electronic communications, the document authors. These people must become proficient in using the hardware and software to produce documents. The second, larger group is all of the other employees, or readers, who must become familiar with the techniques available to them for retrieving communications. The training function can be done either in-house, with consultants, or through a local computer training center. It is, however, critical to have an internal group, such as enduser support (EUS), which will provide assistance with questions that come from employees who create, apply or use electronic communications.

Dr. Greg Voeltz of U S WEST stresses the importance of both the needs analysis and training. He says, "First, there must be a well-established requirement. Second, training—trainers and educators have to understand that they must prepare and teach differently with the tools of electronic communications in an interactive distance, learning situation. Training is essential. When this technology first became available, there was a misconception that it would replace teachers. In fact, this kind of technology requires highly competent teachers, master teachers who can make use of the systems. This technology is not designed to replace face-to-face instruction, but it is an attractive alternative, especially in those locations that cannot afford to bring in educators."

At Eli Lily, system administrators constantly update training efforts to reflect changes that occur with the system or features in the software. Dipak Shah describes this effort: "As administrators, we try to make it easy for end users. We have spent a tremendous amount of money, time and resources on training end users. Periodically, we make them go through training for new or updated features, and we provide on-line manuals."

Initially, the number of information creators will be small in comparison to the number of recipients. The key to success is educating creators to understand that the development of electronic communications is not much different from what they are currently doing. A very simple interface ensures that users don't have to be authoring specialists to create information. The process should be an extension of what they are already doing.

To create useful electronic documents, communicators must learn to think about information in a new way. Scott Johnson has a few basic rules for electronic communicators. He says, "What does a communicator need to do? One, he or she needs to get away from the thought that paper is information. Paper is only a medium that conveys information. The computer is also a medium that delivers information. People associate information with paper. Because the screen is transient, there is the fear that if I turn it off, the information will go away.

"Two, they need to grasp the idea that information is not linear. Just because a book goes from page one to one hundred does not mean that it is one linear stream of information. It is not. In reality, it is 50 or 100 chunks of information, and those chunks have relationships. Information is not continuous, it is discrete. Third, there has to be the idea that we have to accept these new concepts and work with them. Finally, we are going to be able to bring in these data types...multimedia.

"Multimedia is very powerful. If I can call up a video of the corporate president telling me why I'm not getting a raise, that is more powerful than getting a memo across my desk saying I'm not getting a raise. I can look the president in the eye and determine whether he's telling the truth. It may be my assessment, but it's still valuable. I see multimedia as reestablishing intimacy. Fax brought us currency. Electronic mail brought us immediacy, and flattened the bureaucracy. Now, hypertext is bringing us another level at the desktop, and multimedia will let us look people in the eye."

Readers or users must also receive some training, or they will not be able to retrieve and sort information as quickly as possible. Here, the simplest form of training is on-line tutorials that explain to readers how to use the features of the software that may be of benefit to them. HELP functions should be designed into all programs. For training and system design, it is important to consider the percentage of users who have a mouse attached to their computer. Mouse-driven programs can be very different to use than keyboard-controlled programs. If only a few users have mice, and the user interface requires a mouse, the system may fail.

Authors who create documents, readers who look for information and information services personnel who perform system administration each have specific requirements for multimedia software. Table 7-1 identifies some of the requirements that these three groups have, and Table 7-2 compares features of several popular multimedia software packages.

Table 7-1   Comparison of Multimedia Software for Information Systems Staff, Authors and Readers

Information Systems	Authors	Readers
Allows for system security	Manipulate backgrounds	Key word and index searches
Compatible with other software (word processing and graphics)	Create function buttons, i.e., print, search, table of contents	Able to export information to other software on local computer
Works in a LAN environment	Links to various file types (graphic, text, video, audio)	Navigation tools, i.e., history shows where you are

Table 7-1   Comparison of Multimedia Software for Information Systems Staff, Authors and Readers

Information Systems	Authors	Readers
Comes with user/author help system	Manipulate text styles, fonts	Can add reader notes and bookmarks to enhance the information and future use

Table 7-2   Comparison of Hypertext Software Products

Company Product Name	Windows and DOS-Based	Supports ASCII Files	Supports PCX Graphic	Works on Network
AskSam (AskSam Systems)	Yes	Yes	Yes	Yes
BRS Search (BRS Search)	Yes	Yes	Yes	Yes
FolioVIEWS (Folio Corp.)	Yes	Yes	Yes	Yes
Hyperties (Cognetics)	Yes	Yes	Yes	Yes
HyperWriter (NTERGAD)	Yes	Yes	Yes	Yes
MAGGELAN (Lotus Development)	Yes	Yes	Yes	Yes

Once trained, employees will push the technology to accomplish new tasks that make their jobs easier. This has a cascading effect which increases productivity throughout the organization. "The advantage to training people is that they become their own independent thinkers on how to use the systems they have," says Sarah Norton, acknowledging that training pays off for the organization as well as the employee. "People who are properly trained don't just become slaves to the word processor or spreadsheet. They really begin to understand what the great advantages are in these systems. For example, medical offices today are automated to the point where all of their billing is done on a computer system, but there are few medical offices that have their patient information up in systems. There are even fewer that tie patient information right into the hospital where the doctor is on staff. By training medical staff, employees begin to clamor for these capabilities. They quickly understand how to use them effectively so that the productivity gains that business is trying to identify and qualify tend to show up."

The return on investment for training is so great that some organizations insist upon training. Commenting on the subject, Ritch Gaiti at Merrill Lynch says, "You have to require it. It has to be mandatory that people get trained. Managers have to be measured against the fact that their people are trained adequately. You have to start at the management level. Mandate it. Set a reasonable, attainable goal, make sure that people are trained and look for feedback. Then reward people who perform better because they are trained. There is no magic here. It's just doing the job."

Rodger Hutchinson, President of CD-ROM Inc., believes that training brings employees up to the level of job proficiency, but it is the employees who are personally excited about the technology that push applications. He says, "Consider a corporation that has 20,000 employees. How many are computer-literate? And what percentage of the computer-literate employees are using the computer to accomplish a specific task because they are required to do it? Finally, how many are using it because they have an internal sense of enjoyment when they use a tool that provides efficiency and technological growth? It is the people who are genuinely excited about the technology who are most likely to pursue multi-use of the computer."

Let's Standardize

The computer industry has made great strides in creating some global standards for message transmission and hardware configurations. Open system architecture continues to promise compatibility of hardware between manufacturers. Nevertheless, organizations struggle with standards, especially in the area of advanced communications technologies where new hardware moves onto the marketplace daily, and integration of audio, video and graphics is not yet user-friendly.

Addressing the issue of standardization for a client, Martin Nisenholtz of Ogilvy and Mather Direct says, "There are 20 different brands of personal computers and workstations at American Express. The Apples aren't compatible with the PS/2s, and they are not compatible with the AT bus. Companies seek propriety in these systems. They are constantly struggling with whether this system should only run on their platform. If it does, that is a problem because nobody wants to implement it."

Ritch Gaiti echoes these concerns. "Standardization is critical. We are constantly trying to standardize. Unfortunately, there are many standards, and a lot of the technology that exists when you need it is not standard."

PC-based communications provide organizations a mechanism that can help improve employee productivity, quality and morale. The manner in which organizations implement technology plays a pivotal role in determining the ultimate success or failure of the technology. A detailed communications needs analysis is a first step in developing a successful system. Technically, organizations must consider the pros and cons of developing a centralized versus a decentralized system architecture. Similarly, the issue of standardization and compatibility must be addressed early. Communication applications can be cost justified by using existing computer networks and hardware. To take full advantage of the productivity gains that the technology offers, organizations must train and support two significant user groups—communicators and readers.

How They Did It: Case Studies

Good thoughts are no better than good dreams, unless they be executed!

—*Ralph Waldo Emerson (1803–1882),*
Nature

Following are case studies of four organizations—Northern Telecom, Union Carbide, GTE and BASF Corporation—that have successfully implemented electronic communication applications. There are similarities and differences between the applications and approaches taken by these companies. Northern Telecom and Union Carbide distribute information to employees at sites across the country. Technically, they both use a centralized system. Northern Telecom places information onto a CD-ROM disk. Data can be accessed by one user at a stand-alone computer, or by multiple users on a local area network. At Union Carbide and BASF Corporation, information is stored on a hard disk, a file server, and distributed via telecommunication lines to local area networks across the country.

When employees are away from the office, they can access the information through telephone lines.

The application at Northern Telecom focuses on technical documentation, archival information that changes infrequently. Users include both employees and customers. At Union Carbide, the application focuses on the information needs of one specific audience, employees in the health, safety and environmental protection department. Information from the U.S. government's *Federal Register* is updated daily.

When employees at GTE's corporate headquarters turn on their computers Monday morning, they will receive an interactive, multimedia news publication. Using a decentralized approach to distribution, the file for the publication is routed to 17 file servers. Software in each employee's computer retrieves updated documents. Also, BASF Corporation employees at sites across the U.S. can retrieve multimedia documents that contain graphics and digitized images.

Northern Telecom Provides Employees and Customers with Electronic Documentation

Imagine that you are in a hurry and need to find a needle in a haystack. This may be close to the experience that technicians go through when telecommunications switches require repairs. Over the course of a year, technical documentation for a large switch can exceed 100,000 pages.

With 57,000 employees globally and annual revenues of $8.4 billion, Northern Telecom is the world's leading supplier of digital telecommunications switching equipment. Major business areas include central office switching equipment, business communications systems and terminals, transmission equipment, cable and plant. Northern Telecom uses electronic communication to provide employees and customers with digital documentation for these highly technical product lines.

The need for electronic communication came from a desire to fulfill customer requests for user-friendly, paperless documentation. Once a need was established, top management provided the go-ahead to develop and implement the technology. Particularly challenging was the requirement to create a system that accepts data and information from numerous software and hardware platforms, and then provides that information to customers who use a variety of computers. Tony Van Atta, Program Manager of Documentation Information Services for the Helmsman Documentation System at Northern Telecom, oversaw many of the aspects of this system. He describes the development and implementation process.

Background

We developed this product for shipping technical documentation with our switches to our customer base. In the past, when New York Telephone, for example, bought one of our large switches, they got the rights to have 50 feet of paper with it. Then we would send them 30,000 pages three times a year to go along with that switch.

We went through a documentation initiative in which we were getting beaten up by customers for the documentation with our product. They said, "It's too hard to read, you're writing it for a masters-level individual, and you're compounding the problem by giving us more and more paper. You need to rewrite the documents."

What we have done is develop a method by which we can deliver documentation electronically. It delivers integrated text and graphics in a WYSIWYG (What You See Is What You

Get) format to the desktop, regardless of the type of workstation. Users receive full-font, integrated text and graphic representation of the document at their desktop computer.

Implementation

The internal sale was almost nonexistent. Everyone understood that electronic document delivery was the way to go. It was one of those magical things that transpired based on the document initiative in 1985. It had top-down thrust. There was a presidential directive that we change the way we do business with our documentation.

Northern Telecom has always been decentralized. Each division is autonomous because they are close to the customer. They know what to do better than someone sitting at corporate headquarters. At headquarters we manage the global perspective, the strategic planning. This document delivery system is the only project Northern Telecom has ever centralized.

Development

We developed a technical standard for documents that uses many different fonts. It deals with integrated text and graphics. To reduce the number of pages, we focused on using more and more graphics. We explained complex electronics with graphics instead of words.

After we finished that work, we looked for a method to deliver these documents electronically. We found nothing on the market at the time. Vendors said, "This is nice and wonderful, Northern Telecom, but text is going one way, graphics are going the other, and you can never put them together." We developed a way of taking integrated text and graphics from a variety of different authoring packages. For example we had

44 authoring centers authoring documents worldwide using 25 separate authoring packages.

Employees were using everything from Word to Word-Perfect to Interleaf, which is a UNIX-based authoring package. The only thing they had in common was that they all could produce a PostScript file. So PostScript became the common file format with which we took documents into our system. We converted that PostScript file into a hardware-independent file format called CGM (Computer Graphics Metafile). CGM has since become an ISO, or international, standard. CGM is hardware- and media-independent.

So we create our library of documents and put them on one CD-ROM disk. That one CD-ROM disk goes everywhere. It goes to the Macintosh, PC and UNIX environments. In some cases there are UNIX environments that don't read CD-ROM disks, so we put them on a hard drive. Some groups use the CD-ROM as a stand-alone application with one MS-DOS or Mac box attached to a CD-ROM player. In some cases, like New York Telephone, which put it on a hard drive, a node of 300 people access the documents. We put 250,000 pages on one disk.

Most document users are internal. When a customer calls up with a problem they call one of our support centers, which have the documents electronically available. We are also moving into marketing information. This is not the most economical method for distribution of documents that change frequently because the process where we convert PostScript into this hardware-independent file is a batch, off-line process. If you have documents that are changing weekly, this is a problem. If you have documents that change quarterly, it's not a big deal.

Features

Use of color

The file formats are in place so that if you can produce color documents, we can deliver color documents with the system. Our customer base is not completely aware of this, and we haven't broadcast the capability because they would want us to write in color. It was difficult to standardize on 18-point Helvetica bold for title chapters. Now if we have to say titles are blue, what color blue?

Searching

There is a full-phrase, full-text retrieval engine. It includes reader annotations and bookmarks. It also has a print-on-demand capability. You need resident software on your PC to use these features. It requires different applications for the Macintosh, the PC running Microsoft Windows, or the Hewlett Packard or Sun box. We have developed software to do this. To my knowledge, it is the only thing available in the world that allows you to display integrated text and graphics, and if you have words that exist within graphics, you can search on them.

Speed

Northern Telecom has a 10,000-page document. This one document goes with our product line. How quickly do you think you could find something in a 10,000-page document? If you look for it electronically you search for a keyword, and in less than a second you can find the pages you're looking for.

Administration

There is something called the electronic document delivery pyramid. You draw a pyramid on a piece of paper and divide it into thirds. The bottom third of the pyramid is data capture, the middle third is data conversion and indexing, and the top third is document delivery. Until now, the bottom two-thirds of the pyramid have been cost-prohibitive. Those are the two pieces that we automate. We have one full-time person and one part-time person performing the conversion from PostScript to CGM. We distributed two billion pages electronically during 1991 with less than two full-time staff people!

We have two funnels. We have a funnel coming in that is wide open because we are not tied to a specific package, and we have a funnel going out because we are sending CGM everywhere. It's totally automated.

Gatekeeping

Each individual division is responsible for that. They are the purveyors of the data for their product line. In the case of Northern Telecom, there are 13 divisions doing that.

Document Authoring

Internally, the network that is in place to deliver our authoring system is done through an intercorporate network called "CORWAN." In the past, they would have to make their own computer tapes that said Saint Lorans or Research Triangle Park (RTP) and put them on Federal Express. Now, they just copy them across the CORWAN backbone. We are trying to broaden the document base well beyond technical documentation. Now we are looking at marketing information, Northern Telecom practices, anything that would be considered a static document.

User Training

Everyone moving from paper to electronic delivery has to be trained. The systems we use are oriented towards computer mice. I have seen people pick up a mouse and try to use it like a remote control device for a television. There is definitely a need for training. One of the things that we have been able to do is take the 8 1/2" × 11" page that everybody has worked with for the past 2,000 years and put it on the screen. Basically, we take the page off the desk and put it onto the computer.

The Payoffs

There is a tremendous benefit to the bottom line. We save money internally from going from distribution of paper to distribution of electronic information. We also pass that value on to the customer base, who no longer has to have a library in which to hang these 50 feet of documents, and they don't need a librarian managing those documents. There has been a tremendous productivity increase. We have one customer who typically spent four hours from problem identification to resolution. Now they are doing it in 45 minutes.

Union Carbide Delivers *U. S. Federal Register* On-line and On Time

What is going on in the Federal Government?

Some answers to this difficult question can be found by reading the *Federal Register*. Every working day of the year, the Government Printing Office (GPO) publishes this voluminous document, which provides industry and the public with regulations and legal notices issued by federal agencies. Material for the *Register* comes from a variety of sources, including the Department of Education, Department of Energy, Department of Transportation, Environmental Protection Agency, Office of Management and Budget and the National Aeronautic and Space Agency.

Through the course of a year, the *Federal Register* may encompass as many as a quarter of a million pages of information. This is a tremendous amount of information to effectively sort and distribute to employees at different locations. Private industry uses information in the *Federal Register* to examine and comment upon proposed regulations that have an impact upon business. The *Federal Register* is also used to ensure compliance with new regulations. The chemical industry is perhaps more directly affected by information published in the *Federal Register* than other industries. Important rules covering everything from plant emissions to transportation guidelines and occupational safety regulations are covered.

With annual chemical sales topping $4.8 billion, Danbury, Connecticut-based Union Carbide remains one of the top six U.S. chemical companies. Not a small feat, considering the economic impact of the 1984 Bhopal, India, accident— approximately $3 billion spent to defeat a 1985 takeover attempt by GAF and recent divestitures of several business units. Union Carbide Chemicals and Plastics Company continues to operate numerous manufacturing facilities. Compliance with environmental regulations is dependent upon rapid distribution of information to environmental representatives. Gary Whipple, Assistant Director Environmental Affairs, spearheaded a project that sends information from the *Federal Register* to sites across the country, and allows employees to search the information for specific details. Whipple describes the development and implementation of the project.

Background

The audience includes health, safety and environmental professionals at approximately 50 locations across the country, in different divisions, and at headquarters. We started out a couple of years ago to meet several needs. First, users wanted to track compliance-driven activities. We provided a desktop action planner for this purpose. The second thing they wanted was an electronic mail system. We bought DaVinci mail for DOS users and Microsoft Mail for Macintosh users, and have since standardized on Microsoft Mail. The third thing was a desire to place the *Federal Register*, selected Codes of Federal Regulations and our internal guidance on-line in a text searchable format. Users wanted the original, unadulterated text.

Implementation

The first time I proposed putting the *Federal Register* on-line, people laughed at me. They said it was not possible. Those same people became some of the most ardent supporters.

The way we sold the concept involved two steps. First, we had a user survey. We conducted about 120 interviews with plant people, division people and people at headquarters. We asked them what they needed to improve the way they work. What would they like to have in the way of information management systems? We wanted to know how we could help them manage their information. The survey created a six-page laundry list of wants and needs.

Second, our management said, 'Before you ask for money, we want the buy-in of the location and division environmental protection people.' We brought all of these people into a room and spent eight hours making a pitch. What was memorable about this was that everybody got a vote, and the vote was unanimous to proceed. That is a clear message from users to management. From that point on, it was a given that we would get what we needed. Information Services was really not involved. We kept them apprised of what we were doing, but we used commercial software that was network-oriented, and they chose not to be involved.

The *Federal Register* runs about 100,000 pages per year. Every day, the government sends a nine-track tape to the Government Printing Office with that day's *Federal Register* on it. It is loaded with printing codes. A firm, Counterpoint Publishing, receives a copy of the information each evening, processes it through a machine that strips out printing codes, and transfers the ASCII information to our network, where a computer converts the text into FolioViews format and adds a menu, a table of contents and hypertext links. We placed FolioViews on a network here in Danbury, Connecticut. People access that software through either the wide area network or dial-in access.

I was concerned that we would find something that would trip us up. We identified the software that we wanted, but the issue of getting the text into the machine was a big one. We considered putting a person on staff to key it in. Buying the subscription was the right answer for us. The second hurdle was that we have a nonhomogenous computing environment. We have Mac users and DOS users. So we had to find software that not only met the needs of users, but was also available on both platforms. We found a communications package that comes in both Mac and DOS flavors. Users dial in here at high speeds and run on the communications servers. Now that we are expanding to wide area network usage, DOS users are mostly running network operating systems that use

IPX. For Mac users, we are waiting for commercial IPX that will let them get in here.

We have successfully married our e-mail system and the FolioViews application so that a person can create and save a query that they use frequently. For instance, if I am interested in SARA (the Superfund Amendment and Reauthorization Act), I could create a query called "SARA" with those key-words. Every day, I can automatically execute that query without human intervention. It will search through that day's *Federal Register* and send me an e-mail to tell me if there is anything that fits.

Remote access to the system via telephone lines has also been very useful. Although transmission over telephone lines is not as fast as on a local area network, the speed of text trans-mission is more than adequate. I can use remote access if I am in a motel room or at a Chemical Manufacturers Association meeting in Washington or at home. The dial-in speed is faster than you can read. That is largely because we are not transmit-ting the entire file or the executable software over the wire. We use the notebook computer or remote machine as a smart ter-minal. Users have the keyboard and the screen there, but are using the processor here. All of the processing is done here, and only results are shipped over the phone lines.

Administration

Daily we put the complete *Register,* cover to cover, includ-ing IRS and Department of Transportation information, on-line. We have every single *Federal Register* for the past 2-1/2 years stored, and we have selected parts of *Registers* back to the early 70s. Every evening we get a modem-to-modem transmis-sion which contains that day's *Federal Register.* It takes only minutes to place the information on the system and automatically start the ASCII-to-FolioViews conversion.

Features

Searching

FolioViews indexes every number, letter, word and symbol in the original text. Users can search on any of those. That feature appealed to us because people are not limited by someone else indexing the information, so nobody does interpretation or assigns keywords. Users can search by whatever words the government uses.

Graphics

We have on-line illustrations and tables that are in the *Register.*

Training

We retained outside personnel to provide training for staff here in Danbury. We videotaped that in our television theater and edited it into a two-hour training tape which we made available to the location people.

Payoffs

The principal benefit is one that was unforeseen. Previously, we would get a paper copy of the *Federal Register* and draft guidance, and get it out to the sites. That process would take from three to five weeks. We have been successful in getting guidance out to locations within 48 hours of publication of the *Federal Register* in Washington. We don't promise that every day. We promise to get it out within a week.

We have branched out to putting state health, safety and environment regulation information on our system. We plan on putting our own internal policies, procedures and practices manuals on-line. We have had people use the technology to put historical archives of toxicology reports on-line. It is a great tool for laypeople to manage information.

GTE Creates an Interactive Multimedia Publication

News will never be the same. At GTE Corporate Headquarters in Stamford, Connecticut, the Corporate Internal Communications (CIC), Graphics and Information Systems (IMS) departments jointly converted a weekly newsletter into a multimedia publication that incorporates text, graphics, color photographs, animation and sound. Other features, such as two-way interaction via 'electronic coupons' make this LAN-based application an exciting, timely and cost-effective communication vehicle. The electronic publication is in a prototype stage.

With annual revenues exceeding $19 billion, the telecommunications business has been very good to GTE. Approximately 117,000 employees work in telecommunications businesses that include voice, video and data services in local, national and international markets. With this technological orientation, GTE Headquarters uses its existing internal networks to provide employees fiber-optic-delivered computer services.

One of the distribution challenges at GTE's Corporate Headquarters is that employees use both IBM and Macintosh computers. A dual-platform, fiber-optic backbone LAN routes information to 17 file-servers, and then conventional cables route the information to 600 terminals. About 50% of the computers are IBM and 50% Macintosh. With experience developing multimedia presentations for internal customers, the Corporate Internal Communications and Graphic Communications departments became responsible for the design of the electronic publication. Charlie Ernst, Senior Employee Communications Specialist, describes the development of the project.

Background

The GTE Weekly publication provides employees business, education and training, health and employee association news—even a menu from the cafeteria. To save money on printing and distribution while simultaneously improving the timeliness of information, we created an electronic version of the publication.

Several events contributed to the development of this project. First, GTE has an ongoing effort to reduce costs and improve efficiency. Second, our building-wide communications network evolved using both IBM-compatible and Macintosh personal computers. As the company moved to these two platforms, the Graphics department selected Macintosh. And third, we have increasingly been creating computer-based, interactive multimedia for live presentations. Many of these presentations use MacroMedia Director multimedia software to create animated visuals and audio. The visuals consist of text, animation, graphics and some video, and the audio combines voice, sound effects and music. Typical audiences include various internal departments and some external audiences.

Development

The project was developed by a 10-person team, including the Corporate Internal Communications, Graphic Communications and Information Management Systems departments. CIC, Graphics and IMS presented the concept of the electronic publication to senior management. Their response was very positive and supportive, which lead to the development of the prototype newsletter.

One of the publication's parameters was to provide all features of the print version, plus the additional benefits provided by an electronic version. The design challenge was to transform a printed publication to the computer environment that relates to the printed piece. This was accomplished by retaining many of the design elements from the printed version. The electronic version was formatted for a color computer monitor. To replicate the printed publication arriving in the Monday morning mail, the electronic version is programmed to automatically appear on the employees' computers on Monday morning when they turn their computer on. The initial screen will load in approximately eight seconds. We want to ensure that employees can read *The GTE Weekly* immediately or have the ability to quit out of it on their hard drive and store it for later reading if they choose.

We create an interactive aspect to the project, which provides automatic information-gathering. For example, if an employee wants to sign up for a training course presented in the electronic publication, they simply type in their name, click a 'SEND' button, and the information goes back to the person gathering the information.

Distribution

To effectively distribute the publication on our dual platform, we will port MacroMind to the LAN. We will create both a Macintosh and Windows version of the publication each week. The file size is about 750 kilobytes. To minimize peak load on the network, the IMS staff will send it over the network on Friday evening, where it resides on the 17 file servers. The program then duplicates itself.

A 'player' version of the document will reside on the hard disk of employees' computers. When users click on an icon, the software will pull down the data for that week's document. This improves speed and file size capability.

Internal Communications will continue to write and edit the information that is delivered, and the graphics department will design and produce the publication—as well as the navigational aspects, and the Information Management Systems staff will provide technical support, particularly in the area of distribution.

It has taken approximately a year to develop this system. We have the electronic document, and we know how to distribute it. We are currently piloting the electronic news publication on a single floor. We want to make sure this works perfectly before we distribute it to all employees. We will eventually completely eliminate the hard copy when we go electronic.

Timeliness

Virtually instantaneous distribution replaces printing the publication and conventional mail room distribution.

Features

Electronic Coupon

The electronic coupon works. We may have an article about a CPR training course. A reader interested in taking the class types in their name, and the system automatically sends the information back to the health and safety department.

Printing

Users can print out individual stories.

Security

Once it is authored, readers cannot alter the file.

Colors

The color palette is 256 colors because we use both IBM and Macintosh platforms (versus black-and-white print version).

Technology

Uses existing technology and promotes GTE's core business of telecommunications. The publication is easy to use and does not require sophisticated computer knowledge.

Administration

Internal communications will continue to write and edit *The GTE Weekly.* It takes about five to ten hours to produce the electronic document each week. Information Management Systems ensures that the publication is distributed effectively through the LAN.

Training

The document creators are already familiar with the software. Since the publication is easy to use, employees can literally be trained to use this program in a couple of minutes. The publication has a simple bulletin tutorial. We feel it is essential that the electronic document is user-friendly for readers. This is important because we have a diverse group of users—some are infrequent computer users, and some are very sophisticated computer users.

Payoffs

In addition to reducing the cost and time involved in producing the publication, this project will reduce the amount of paper that we distribute. We are spearheading this at the Corporate Headquarters and are finding that the different GTE business units are interested in this as well. Each operating unit can tailor this system to their specific applications.

BASF 'Information Server' Provides Multimedia Documents to Desk-top PCs

BASF is a diversified manufacturer of chemicals and chemical-based materials headquartered in Germany. Through the 1980s BASF Corporation expanded rapidly in the United States and Canada, acquiring several businesses, and growing to encompass five divisions with more than 16,000 employees at 40 major production sites.

Background

In the early 1990s computers came into widespread use at BASF in the U.S. and Canada. Local-area and wide-area network connections grew rapidly, and X.400 gateways allowed electronic mail to be delivered easily between sites. In 1992, more than 5,000 employees at sites across the country were connected to a wide area network (by 1994 the number increased to over 7,000). Aware that the network infrastructure would allow information to be transmitted to a large audience, the Corporate Communications department joined forces with the MIS department to sponsor the development of an electronic communications system—an Information Server—which would provide LAN-connected employees with a variety of multimedia information at their desktop PCs.

Development

Senior management recognized that Information Server offered benefits that would quickly outweigh start-up costs. The catalyst for the project was the desire to transform one internal publication, a newsletter for managers, into a strictly electronic publication. BASF realizes cost savings from a reduction in paper production (printing and copying) and paper distribution (mail and interoffice) using this electronic communication system to communicate a wide variety of topics to employees.

There are other benefits as well. By sharing information with employees at all levels of the organization the project would simultaneously strengthen the corporate culture and develop new 'synergies' as employees and managers learn what other departments are doing. Business strategies benefit through the distribution of news about the competition.

There are other communication applications. Press releases, ranging from new product announcements to acquisitions, sales and earnings, are issued electronically. Although releases are distributed via a wire service to the media, and senior managers receive all relevant releases by fax machines, placing releases on the Information Server enables employees to receive company news internally, rather than from outside sources.

The document creators at BASF represent departments throughout the organization, and the audience includes every employee connected to a local area network tied into the central file server.

Implementation

To implement the system technically, Information Systems appointed a project manager to work in cooperation with a manager from Corporate Communications. It was recognized that other departments, including Human Resources, Treasury, Finance and Information Services (to name a few), had information and communications that could effectively be distributed to a broad audience. A series of interviews were set up with vice presidents of all major corporate functions. The interviews provided information needed to define technical requirements. They also increased multidepartment support for the project. Departments involved included:

- Communications
- Ecology
- Engineering
    Engineering
    Capital Management
    Construction Engineering
- Finance
- Human Resources
    Field
    Staff
        Benefits
        Medical
        Training
        Staffing
        Industrial Relations
- Information Services
- Legal
    Tax
    Insurance

Regulatory Affairs

Legal Services

➤ Travel

➤ Treasury

The interview process focused on identifying the types of documents that each department would find useful for distribution and the features that users would need to make the system functional and user-friendly. After the user requirements were clearly defined, the project team began to research commercially available software products that could meet those requirements. The technological review required that software meet several criteria. The software had to provide hypertext capabilities for linking files in a non-linear fashion and needed word processing features for easy creation by users, the interface had to be DOS-based, and the product had to offer run-time versions for readers.

After a review of more than 30 different products the company selected HyperWriter software from Connecticut-based NTERGAID. In addition to attractive author and reader features, the company offers free run-time versions of the software. As a result, reader software is installed directly on the file servers of local area networks. This allows all employees to receive the data, and speeds up transmission time. Hyper-Writer (version 3.1) allows support for Microsoft Windows, as well as DOS, using the same database. Windows, with its WYSIWYG (What You See Is What You Get) printing improves printing capability (including Harvard Graphics data), also more data types are supported.

The information systems staff had established criteria for the project to ensure that the system would be easy to install and administer, and friendly for users. These included:

➤ Use existing network infrastructure

➤ Keep technical administration low

➤ Provide a common document surface

➤ Make the system easy to use

➤ Use existing network speed (keep response time to a minimum)

As a result of the criteria, the decision was made to install executable reader software on remote LANs, and use one central file server for document creation and storage.

Building The Information Server

The Information Server uses a central system architecture. Initially, the Information Server consisted of one file server located in New Jersey, a 486-MHz PC with 26 megabytes of RAM and 4 gigabytes of hard disk space.

The telecommunications lines to different BASF sites across the country have different line speeds. Thus, a reader at a site with faster line speed would receive the information faster than a reader at a site with slower line speed. The other factor in response time relates to how large the files are that need to be sent to the reader. Hardware and software needed to be tested. Tests were run to five different sites with line speeds ranging from 56 kilobytes per second to 1.5 megabytes per second. File sizes ranging from 5k to 25k were then transmitted to each of these sites and carefully timed. It was determined that by limiting the size of a 'topic' to 5 - 10k, readers at sites with T1 lines would normally receive information in less than 4 seconds, and sites with the slowest transmission speeds would still receive adequate response time of less than 15 seconds.

Initial testing indicated transmission speeds could support access to the data across the company's network. However, the number one request from users was for improved response time. As a result, it was determined to provide a one-time download of the data to each LAN file server on the network. Approximately 40 Mb is required to store the data on each server. This allows users to view data at the speed of access to their **local** file server. This improvement to the Information Server system increases usage and allows for greater use of graphics (which are inherently slow to display.) Daily updates are sent to each file server across the network, thereby keeping all copies of the Information Server data current.

To address Corporate Communications' goal of reaching employees without personal computers, touch screen terminals (housed in kiosks) are being placed in open areas. Now in the pilot stage, the kiosks allow an employee to query the Information Server without using a keyboard, mouse or switches. Security concerns are addressed by placing the kiosks in secured areas of the company.

Features

Searching

In the future users will be able to perform full text retrieval with key-word searching. For example, in an issue of *Management Information* or *Business Information News,* a reader would select a 'Search' button and type in 'automotive.' All of the stories that contain the word automotive will be located.

Printing

The print button lets readers print out the on-screen information at a local printer (with the exception of Harvard Graphics data which does not print under DOS).

Color and Graphics

Hyperwriter offers a wide range of color options, dependent primarily upon the user's monitor. Color .PCX, .GIF and .TIFF graphics can be imported into documents.

Security

Any employee with a LAN-based computer can access the information. However, document authors, referred to as document owners, require security passwords to add or change documents on the system.

Because of the large reader audience it is assumed that the information can reach the general public, even the media. Therefore, only non-confidential information, which was already distributed to a significant portion of employees, is appropriate for inclusion on the Information Server.

Corporate Communications reviews requests from departments, or individuals who want to put information on the Information Server. After a document author is approved, no further review of the application or their documents is required. Each author is a document owner, just as they are in paper form, and maintain all responsibility for the content. With input from legal and security departments, guidelines for material and system administration were established in a formal policy statement.

Training

Ten document authors were selected for a pilot of the Information Server. These authors attended a software training session developed by the software manufacturer, tailored to the technical specifications of the BASF system. An on-line hypertext tutorial provides first-time readers information on how to navigate in the system and explains the features, such as printing. Authors also could use a software tutorial to answer questions. BASF end user support provides assistance to authors and readers.

Administration

The system requires little technical administration. Local LAN administrators must initially set up their LANs to accept data from the Information Server and make the Information Server a menu choice for employees. Document authors create documents either on-line or on local PCs, and then download to the Information Server. New items on the main menu are updated as needed.

Payoffs

Corporate Communications uses the Information Server to distribute a wide variety of information including:

- ➤ Daily Business News—a synopsis of newspaper articles on topics of importance to the company and its businesses.
- ➤ Daily Financial News—including currency conversion rates.
- ➤ Organizational directory.
- ➤ Monthly management newsletter.
- ➤ Press releases and internal announcements.
- ➤ Corporate policies, procedures and guidelines including purchasing, human resources, financial, safety and loss prevention and record retention.
- ➤ Summaries of federal statues applicable to business units.
- ➤ Corporate training courses and schedules.

➤ Quality issues.

➤ Surplus equipment availability catalog.

➤ Travel—a hotel directory and car rental information.

On an annual basis, BASF Corporation saves more than the cost of the system in the reduction and distribution of paper. Add the value of timely information retrieval by employees throughout the United States and Canada, and the Information Server is a tremendous success.

Glossary of Terms

ANSI American National Standards Institute. A nonprofit, privately funded membership organization. Founded in 1918, ANSI coordinates the development of U.S. voluntary national standards in both the private and public sectors. ANSI is the U.S. member body to the International Standards Organization (ISO) and the International Electrotechnical Commission (IEC).

ASCII Acronym for American Standard Code for Information Interchange. It is a standard coding scheme that assigns numeric values to text and control characters, thereby achieving compatibility among different computer systems. ASCII data is free of any special formatting codes.

ASYNC Asynchronous communications. This is a way to transmit data in which start and stop bits are used to frame each character. Most modems for personal computers are asynchronous.

Backbone   In telecommunications, a backbone is the portion of a network that handles the majority of the traffic.

Bandwidth   In networking, bandwidth refers to the transmission capacity of a communications channel— higher bandwidths allow for faster data transmission.

Baud Rate   The switching speed of a line, equivalent to the number of changes in the electrical state of the line per second. Baud rate is equivalent to bits per second at low speeds. For example, 300 baud is the same as 300 bits per second (bps). At higher speeds, the bits per second is greater than the baud rate, because one baud can be made to represent more than one bit.

BBS   Bulletin board system. A computer that usually operates 24 hours a day and provides a forum for information exchange. A variety of services, such as screen bulletins, file transfer and electronic mail, are usually offered.

Binary   A file transfer mode that transmits any type of file without loss of data.

BIT   The smallest unit of information that a computer can read. Eight bits are used to make one alphanumeric character, such as the letter "A." These eight characters make up a "BYTE."

BPS   Bits Per Second. Used to measure the speed of data transfer in a communications system.

Byte   The amount of space that is needed to make up one alphanumeric character, such as the letter "B."

CD-ROM Acronym for compact disc-read only memory. This is a high-capacity optical storage device that can store approximately 600 MB of information (the equivalent of almost 300,000 pages of text).

Client-Server A computing architecture that distributes processing between clients (desk-top PCs that request information from the server) and servers (usually PCs with greater hard-disk space that store data and programs shared by many clients).

COM1,2,3,4 The name assigned to serial ports on a personal computer. COM ports are usually connected to a modem, mouse or serial printer.

Computer-Based Training (CBT) The application and use of computers to deliver instruction and training, and often to record and tally student testing results.

Computer Graphics Metafile (CGM) A file format for the transfer of device-independent computer graphics between computer systems. A metafile contains both the image and instructions for recreating the image.

Data Compression Encoding data to take up less space.

Download Transferring files from one computer to another over a network or using a modem.

Downlink Transmission from a satellite to an earth station.

Duplex In an asynchronous transmission it is the ability to transmit and receive on the same channel simultaneously. This is also called 'full-duplex.'

Dynamic Data Exchange A method by which computer software programs communicate with each other.

Electronic Mail   E-mail. Using a network or a modem to send messages from one computer to another. E-mail can also include attachments, which are often other files, such as spreadsheets.

Emulation   Terminal emulation allows different kinds of computers to talk to each other (PCs talk to mainframes).

Ethernet   A network protocol and cabling scheme that has a transfer rate of 10 megabits per second. Ethernet was developed by Xerox in 1976.

Expert System   A problem-solving or decision-making system that uses information derived from a human expert to help a user find information or even solutions. It is a form of artificial intelligence.

Export   To transfer (in ASCII or text form) information from a computer program to a disk file for future use.

FAX   Abbreviation for facsimile. A machine that electronically transmits copies of documents to a receiving machine, where they are reproduced.

Fiber Distributed Data Interface (FDDI)   This is a specification for fiberoptic networks that transmit at a speed of up to 100 megabits per second.

Fiber Optic Cable   Cable that transmits signals by sending pulses of light. In addition to sending data at the speed of light, fiber optic cable is immune to electrical interference.

File Server   A networked computer that is used to store files and programs which are accessed by other client computers on the network.

File Transfer   Moving files from one computer to another.

File Transfer Protocol (FTP)   A technique that allows the transmission of one or more files from one computer to another. This protocol divides a file into small units which are processed in sequence.

Gateway   In a network, a gateway is a shared connection between the local area network and a larger system, which could be a mainframe computer or a packet-switching network.

Groupware   Software that works on a network and allows numerous users to work on projects simultaneously, sharing ideas and information.

Hypertext   A technique for presenting information in such a way that readers can access the information in a nonsequential fashion, jumping from point-to-point.

Information Superhighway   The catch phrase that describes the developing telecommunications system that will transmit interactive video, voice and data into the homes of millions of people.

Internet   A global telecommunications network that connects more than 15 million users in at least 60 countries. Internet uses TCP/IP protocols.

Kermit   An asynchronous communications protocol for PCs developed at Columbia University and used in public-domain communications programs. Kermit is a slow protocol but offers transmission accuracy over noisy telephone lines.

Leased Line   A telephone line or a communications circuit that is reserved for the permanent use of a specific customer.

Local Area Network (LAN)   A group of computers connected by a communication channel. The LAN allows files and programs to be shared between several users.

Metafile   A file that has information related to other files. A graphics metafile, for example, contains a graphic image and information that details how the image should be displayed.

Modem   A modulator/demodulator. It is a device that links computers via telephone lines.

Multimedia   Computer technologies that provide users with images, audio and text, often in an interactive fashion.

Multiplexing   A method for transmitting several signals simultaneously over a communications channel.

Noise   Unwanted signals on a communication channel that degrade the quality of the signal.

On-line Service   A commercial or non-commercial service that provides users access to a variety of files and data-bases as well as messaging opportunities.

Port   An external connector on a computer. It is used to hook up a modem, printer or other device. Data enters and leaves the computer via a serial port during a tele-communications session. Sometimes referred to as the COM port, this is where an RS-232 cable connects an external modem to the computer.

Protocol   A set of rules and regulations that govern transmitting and receiving of data.

RS-232   25-wire electrical cable used between a computer and a peripheral device such as a modem, mouse or printer.

SYNC Synchronous communications. A method of communications in which a group of characters are sent as a continuous stream of data at regular intervals.

SYSOP System's operator. The individual who maintains the operation of an electronic bulletin board or forum. Their duties include upgrading software, updating files, backing up the system and ensuring the security of the data.

Telecommunications The transmission or reception of data using any electromagnetic means, such as a computer.

Telecommuting Working from home or a remote location by using a computer that is connected to the main office.

Upload Transferring file from a remote computer to a host computer.

V.42 A standard for modem error correction.

Videodisc An optical disk that can store images and sound—the equivalent of 55,000 still images or two hours of full-motion video.

Wide Area Network (WAN) The extension of a local area network. A WAN connects users across very large distances and often connects users at multiple sites.

Wordwrap A feature of text handling systems that makes text drop down one line and start again at the left margin when a line of text is full.

Sources

Listing of companies and organizations should not be taken as an endorsement or recommendation. Information was accurate at the time of writing, but the writer and publisher cannot be responsible for omissions, errors or changes that occur after compilation of these sources.

Professional Organizations

American Library Association
50 East Huron Street
Chicago, IL 60611
(312) 944-6780
Contact: Dr. Peggy Sullivan, Executive Director

American Society for Information Science
8720 Georgia Avenue
Suite 501
Silver Spring, MD 20910-3602
(301) 495-0900
Contact: Richard B. Hill, Executive Director

Association for Information and Image Management
1100 Wayne Avenue
Suite 1100
Silver Spring, MD 20910-5603
(301) 587-8202
Contact: Sue Wolk, Executive Director

Copyright Clearance Center
222 Rosewood Drive
Danvers, MA 01923
(508) 750-8400
Contact: Joseph Alen, President and CEO

Electronic Messaging Association
1655 N. Fort Myer Drive
Arlington, VA 22209
(703) 524-5550
Contact: Bill Moroney, Executive Director

Information Industry Association
555 New Jersey Avenue NW
Suite 800
Washington, DC 20001
(202) 639-8262
Contact: Ken Allen, President

International Interactive Communications Society
14657 SW Teal Blvd. S. 119
Beaverton, Or 97007
(503) 579-IICS
Contact: Debbie Palm, Managing Director

International Television Association (ITVA)
6311 N. O'Connor Road
Suite 230
Irving, TX 75039
(214) 869-1112
Contact: Fred Wehrli, Executive Director

Optical Publishing Association
P. O. Box 21268
Columbus, OH 43221
(614) 442-8805
Contact: Richard Bowers, Executive Director

Society for Applied Learning Technology
50 Culpepper Street
Warrenton, VA 22186
(703) 347-0055
Contact: Raymond Fox, President

Government Agencies

NTIA
National Telecommunications and Information
  Administration
U.S. Department of Commerce
Room 4625
14th Street and Constitution Avenue NW
Washington, DC 20230
(202) 482-1551

NSF
National Science Foundation
4201 Wilson Blvd.
Arlington, VA 22230
(703) 306-1234

Publications

Advanced Imaging
445 Broad Hollow Road
Melville, NY 11747
(516) 845-2700

Boardwatch
8500 W. Bowles Ave
Suite 210
Littleton, CO 80123
(800) 933-6038

BYTE
One Phoenix Mill Lane
Peterborough, NH 03458
(603) 924-9281
BIX - editors, MCI Mail (250-0135)

CD-ROM Professional
462 Danbury Road
Wilton, CT 06897
(203) 761-1466

CD-ROM World
11 Ferry Lane West
Westport, CT 06880
(203) 226-6967

Data Communications/McGraw-Hill
1221 Avenue of the Americas
New York, NY 10020
(212) 512-2699
MCI Mail (416-2157), Internet (416-2157@mcimail.com)

DATAMATION Magazine
275 Washington Street
Newton, MA 02158
(617) 964-3030

On-line Review
Learned Information Ltd.
Woodside, Hinksey Hill
Oxford OX1 5AU, UK
44 (0) 865-730275

Information Week
CMP Publications
600 Community Drive
Manhasset, NY 11030
(516) 562-5000

LAN
600 Harrison Street
San Francisco, CA 94107
(415) 905-2200

Mobile Office
21800 Oxnard Street, Suite 250
Woodland Hills, CA 91367
Fax: (818) 593-6153, CompuServe (76646,3722)

Online Access
900 N Franklin
S. 310 Chicago, IL 60610
(312) 573-1700

PC Computing
950 Tower Lane, 19th Floor
Foster City, CA 94404
(415) 578-7000
MCI Mail (350-2648), CompuServe (7600,21)

PC World
501 Second Street #600
San Francisco, CA 94107
(415) 243-0500

Publish
501 Second Street
San Francisco, CA 94107
(415) 978-3280

Technology Review
MIT Building W59
201 Vassar Street
Cambridge, MA 02139
(617) 253-8250

The Futurist
World Future Society
7910 Woodmont Avenue
S. 450
Bethesda, MD 20814
(301) 656-8274

THE Journal—Technological Horizons In Education
150 El Camino Real
Suite 112
Tustin, CA 92680-3670
(714) 730-4011

Software and Service Providers

Electronic Mail: Software and Services

Advantis
P.O. Box 30021
Tampa, FL 33630
(800) 284-5849

AT&T—EasyLink and AT&T Mail
400 Interpace Parkway
Parsippany, NJ 070545
(800) 62405672

Beyond Incorporated
17 New England Executive Park
Burlington, MA 01803
(617) 229-0006

Futurus
Futurus Corporation
211 Perimeter Center Parkway #910
Atlanta, GA 30346
(404) 392-7979

Lotus Notes
Lotus Development Corporation
400 Riverpark Drive
North Reading, MA 01864
(800) 346-1305

MCI Global Messaging Service
1133 19th Street NW
Washington, DC 20036
(202) 833-8484
Sign Up: (800) 444-6245

Microsoft Mail
Microsoft Corporation
One Microsoft Way
Redmond, WA 98052
(800) 426-9400

On Technology
1 Cambridge Center
Cambridge, MA 02142
(617) 734-4317

Executive Information Systems

Pilot Software
One Canal Park
Cambridge, MA 02141
(617) 374-9400

Cognos Corporation
67 South Bedford Street
Suite 200W
Burlington, MA 01803
(617) 229-6600

Groupware

Group Logic
1408 North Fillmore Street
Suite 10
Arlington, VA 22201
(703) 528-1555

Lotus Notes
Lotus Development Corporation
400 Riverpark Drive
North Reading, MA 01864
(800) 346-1305

Hypertext

AskSam Systems
P.O. Box 1428
Perry, FL 32347
(800) 327-5726

Cognetics
Post Office Box 386
Princeton Junction, NJ 08550
(609) 799-5005

Folio Corporation
2155 North Freedom Blvd.
Suite 150
Provo, UT 84604
(800) 873-3654

Macromedia
600 Townsend Street
Suite 310W
San Francisco, CA 94103
(415) 252-2000

NTERGAID
60 Commerce Park
Milford, CT 06460
(203) 882-0838

Workflow and Electronic Forms

Beyond Incorporated
17 New England Executive Park
Burlington, MA 01803
(617) 229-0006

Delrina Corp.
6830 Via Del Oro #240
San Jose, CA 95119
(800) 268-6082

FileNet Corporation
3565 Harbor
Costa Messa, CA
(714) 966-3400

JetForm Corp.
Watermill Center
800 South St. #305
Waltham, MA 021554
(800) 538-3676

Microsoft Corporation
One Microsoft Way
Redmond, WA 98052
(800) 426-9400

Sigma Imaging Systems
622 Third Avenue, 30th Floor
New York, NY 10017
(212) 476-3000

ViewStar Corporation
1101 Marina Village Parkway
Alameda, CA 94501
(510) 865-7827

WordPerfect Corp.
1555 N. Technology Way
Orem, UT 84057
(800) 228-5077

On-Line Services

America Online
8619 Westwood Center Drive
Vienna, VA 22182-2285
(703) 448-8700
Sign Up: (800) 827-6364

BRS Information Technologies
8000 Westpark Drive
McLean, VA 22102
(703) 442-0900

CompuServe Information Service
P.O. Box 20212
Columbus, OH 43220
(614) 457-0802
Sign Up: (800) 848-8199

Desktop Data, Inc.
601 Trapelo Road
Waltham, MA 02154
(617) 890-0042

Dialog Information Services
3460 Hillsview Avenue
Palo Alto, CA 94303
(800) 334-2564

Dow Jones News/Retrieval
Dow Jones and Company
P.O. Box 300
Princeton, NJ 08543
(609) 452-1511

GEnie
General Electric Information Services
401 N. Washington St.
Rockville, MD 20850
(301) 251-6415
Sign Up: (800) 638-9636

Nexis
Mead Data Central
9443 Springboro Pike
P.O. 933
Dayton, OH 45401
(513) 865-6800

Prodigy
445 Hamilton Avenue
White Plains, NY 10601
(914) 993-8000
Sign Up: (800) 776-3449

Industry Research, Consultation and Implementation

Bill Eager
Electronic Communications Consultant
8522 Martin Lane
Conifer, CO 80433
(303) 674-2107

D/J Brush Associates
Clapp Hill Road
Lagrangeville, NY 12540
(914) 227-8600

Business Research Group
275 Washington Street
Newton, MA 02158-1630
(617) 630-3900

Documentation Development Inc.
520 Eighth Avenue
22nd Floor
New York, NY 10018
(212) 594-8001

Ernst & Young
Center for Information Technology and Strategy
One Walnut Street
Boston, MA 02108
(617) 742-2500

SRI International
333 Ravenswood Avenue
Menlo Park, CA 94025
(415) 326-6200

Videoconferencing

ABL Engineering
6111 Heisley Road
Menor, OH
(216) 974-8585

Intel Corp.
Santa Clara, CA
(800) 538-3373

Northern Telecom
Richardson, TX
(800) NORTHERN

PictureTel
222 Rosewood Drive
Danvers, MA
(508) 762-5000

Silicon Graphics
2011 N. Shoreline Blvd.
Mountain View, CA 94043
(800) 800-7441

Videostar
3490 Piedmont Road
Atlanta, GA 30305
(404) 262-1555

Vitel Corp.
108 Wild Basin Road
Austin, TX 78746
(800) 284-8871

Index

W

X